CASTING CALL

Fly fishing the world with history's largest outdoor television producer and his friends

CASTING CALL

By **Chris Dorsey**

Library of Congress Cataloging-in-Publication Data
Dorsey, Chris.
     Casting Call./Chris Dorsey—1st ed.
      p. cm.
     ISBN 978-1735541525
         1. Fly fishing. 1. Title

Book and cover design by David Kirby, Creative Connection
Printed in Canada by Friesens Publishing
Photographs by John MacGillivray, Dusan Smetana, Marcos Furer,
     Francois Botha, R. Valentine Atkinson, Todd & Brad Reed
Cover photograph by John MacGillivray

Published by Wild River Press, Post Office Box 13360, Mill Creek, Washington 98082 USA

"This collection highlights the writer's uncanny ability to see, appreciate and report on what makes the spirit soar... and what brings a tear."

—from the Foreword by Flip Pallot

Most of the world is covered in water.
A fisherman's job is simple, pick out
the best parts. —Charles Waterman

Advance Praise

I am an angler who has fished every continent except Antarctica, which I believe qualifies me to say that when I read Chris Dorsey's *Casting Call*, it made me feel like I had returned to many of the places I had fished years ago. Chris has the same knack of painting a picture through the written word that Ernest Hemingway possessed—and it makes you feel like you are actually there when you read his stories. If you're looking for a fascinating and interesting read, *Casting Call* is a keeper. — STU APTE, author, *Of Winds and Tides*

If you are looking for destinations to add to your fly-fishing bucket list, there are few people as qualified as Chris Dorsey to be your source. He's a top-notch angler and world-class film maker, and over the years he has seen many of the destinations that are merely a fantasy to most of us. So, if he devoted a chapter to a location in this book, you know you can confidently add it to your list. Much more than a guide book, this is a love story to some of the world's most amazing places, told in ways that are a joy to read. — TOM ROSENBAUER, author, *The Orvis Fly Fishing Guide*

When the legendary fly fisherman Lefty Kreh begins a fishing story in Chris Dorsey's terrific book, with the opening line, "I remember fishing with Castro and Hemingway in Cuba," well, I was hooked! As a basically competent fly fisherman, I read this book with glee and not a little envy. The individual stories of famous and not so famous people hoping to achieve "tight lines" on various rivers and flats across the world had me salivating. Dorsey's passion for fishing, for saving our environment and waters where fish live is beyond commendable. He's a hero. Do read this book. Among its many attributes, it gives serious pause for thought regarding our planet, our waterways and how we all can strive to make it better. This is a must read! — LIAM NEESON, Academy Award Winner

Chris Dorsey's angling life is global. The lucid descriptions of the lands, waters, guides and his own family members keep his book from being the usual self-aggrandizing fare of the angler abroad. It is instead an angler's celebration. I put his book down with the feeling that I'd been on these wonderful outings with him.
— THOMAS McGUANE, author, *The Longest Silence*

Chris Dorsey knows what he's writing about. He is an expert fly fisherman and outdoorsman—and he's fished almost everywhere. He's also a talented writer and, as such, describes the excitement of fishing about as well as anyone I've ever read. If you fly fish, you'll love this book, and if you don't, you will want to after reading it.
— HUEY LEWIS, Grammy Award Winner

Advance Praise

When it comes to hunting and fishing, Chris Dorsey has done it all—or at least most of it. He's pursued his chosen sport the world over and has enjoyed every minute of it and writes about it in ways that make those who haven't had the same experiences feel as if they were there with him. At the same time, he is always aware that the game he pursues and the land and water in which it lives are constantly threatened by greed, thoughtlessness and those who prioritize other interests. He worries even as he celebrates his adventures that our children and grandchildren may never experience them unless we are prepared to defend that which makes it all possible. — DAVID KEENE, *Washington Times*

Chris Dorsey's excellent book, *Casting Call*, jolted my memory bank of all the great fish we chase and the spectacular, fragile places they call home. It made me happy and proud to be an angler of the world, and someone like Chris who is relentless in the fight for their survival! — ANDY MILL, author, *A Passion for Tarpon*

Having been on a few trips with the peripatetic Chris Dorsey, his passion for fly fishing—from his backyard to globetrotting to remote locations around the world—will surely engage you with his unique perspective as he shares his adventures in pursuit of fish and memories. Kick back and vicariously immerse yourself into this global fly-fishing odyssey as he regales you with artfully crafted stories of places and people you may know. Along the way, he'll fuel your own passion to seek new locations that you will most assuredly want to add to your own bucket list. — BILL KLYN, Patagonia

If you are going to create sporting art, you must live the experience or you cannot be authentic. When I read Chris Dorsey's *Casting Call*, it was clear that he was drawn to waters for many of the same reasons they attracted me: the fishing, the beauty of the places and the inspiration that they bring. While this book takes you to remarkable rivers, lakes and flats across the globe, it is as much an insightful journey into the heart of fly fishing as it is a celebration of destinations. While I might work on canvas and Dorsey in words, I was comforted to learn that we share the same love of waters and fish that is central to the spirit of all fly fishermen. — ARTHUR SHILSTONE, *Flashes in the River*

In *Casting Call*, Chris Dorsey takes us on a rollicking tour of some of the most beautiful—and coveted—angling destinations on earth. From Bristol Bay, Alaska to the trout streams of Patagonia, Chris brings to life the kind of places most fishermen dream about. Chris is a true outdoorsman and he knows his subject. Add his wry sense of humor and mix in a cast of characters ranging from Tom Brokaw to Yvonne Chouinard, and you have all the ingredients for a fast-paced and amusing narrative. — GUIDO RAHR, President, Wild Salmon Center

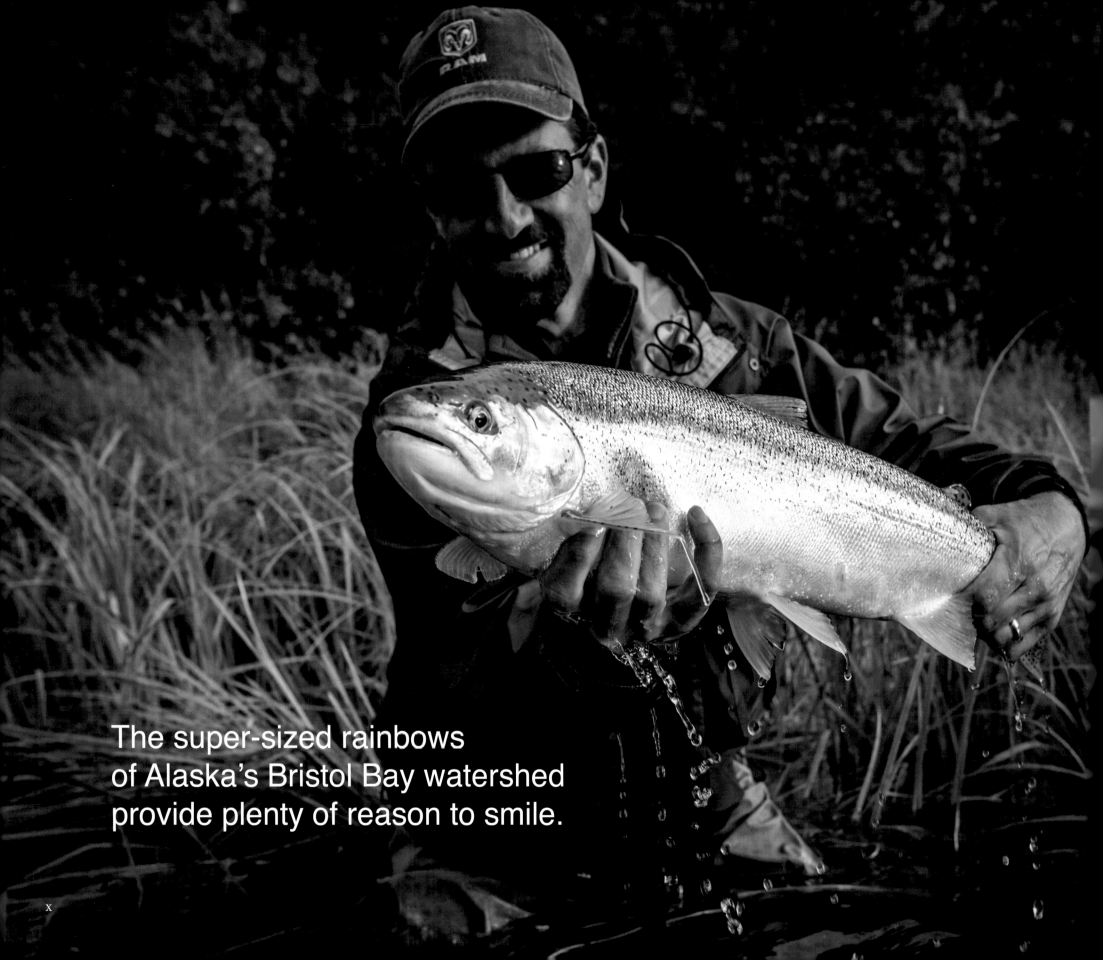

The super-sized rainbows
of Alaska's Bristol Bay watershed
provide plenty of reason to smile.

CONTENTS

Ice Out
Endless days amid the planet's richest fisheries

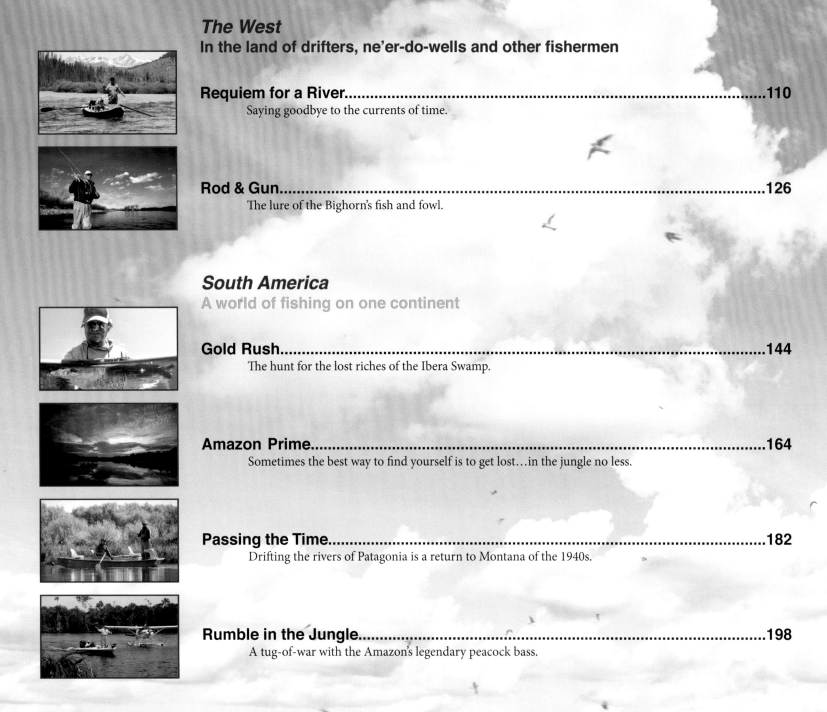

The West
In the land of drifters, ne'er-do-wells and other fishermen

South America
A world of fishing on one continent

The Flats
Double haul adventures in Listerine waters

Amy Dorsey mines
for Alaskan silvers.

A golden dorado takes flight lessons in Argentina's Ibera Swamp.

If I fished only to capture fish, my fishing trips would have ended long ago.
—Zane Grey

Dedication

For Matt Connolly, conservation visionary, mentor and friend with whom I've shared some of the world's great fly waters, and who makes every voyage memorable.

Lefty—The Keeper

He was born to fish,
Lessons savored as a dish.
His shadow still looms,
Because he lived as a bloom.
Gone to the hereafter,
Leaving echoes of laughter.
He casts no more,
Our memories an encore.

Lefty has Brokaw, McGuane
and Keaton in stitches...again.

Lefty Overheard

You're in more trouble than a pregnant nun.

I remember when women wore earrings and men had tattoos.

A baby makes noise at one end and has no responsibility at the other.

A woman thinks you are a genius until you marry her and then you don't know a thing.

There is more BS in fly fishing than a feedlot.

They have streets named after you . . . they call them "one way."

Love is blind and marriage is an eye opener.

God can put you on 'em . . . but he can't catch 'em for you.

The fishing was so good it was like rolling a wine bottle into a jail cell.

She's so ugly the tide wouldn't take her out.

He's so lazy he married a pregnant woman.

He's got as many friends as an alarm clock.

He's so dumb he picked up a snake to kill a stick.

He's spookier than a cat in a dog pound.

He's got more balls than a bowling alley.

He's tougher than a bad mother-in-law.

He could have fun at a funeral.

Upon hearing a story of the one that got away: Why don't you tell me about the three bears too . . . I like fairy tales.

I'll tell you the same thing Marc Anthony told Cleopatra when he snuck into her tent . . . I'm not here to give a speech.

If you are looking for sympathy, this is the wrong boat.

If you can't have fun with Huey Lewis, you belong in a cemetery.

My idea of a rock star is a guy named Jack who looks like a Jill and smells like a John.

If you have problems, think about doing things the opposite way. That works in fishing *and* marriage.

Flip Pallot and Lefty Kreh, brothers of the flats.

Back Casts

You and I are readers, or we wouldn't be here...but I'm ahead of you. I've read this book, and I've read the wingshooting book that Chris Dorsey wrote before this one and wondered, why the long interval between the two?

As you read *Casting Call* that riddle will explain itself. You'll realize, as I did, that only the passage of time, and the gaining of experience, could have paved the way for a collection such as you have before you.

In the spell between books, the production of films and a unique relationship with the natural world, have provided the bedrock for *Casting Call*.

Not simply a narrative of a film producer's adventures, this collection highlights the writer's uncanny ability to see, appreciate and report what makes the spirit soar...and what brings a tear. From the blistering, drag screaming first run of bonefish, to the death of a Rocky Mountain trout stream; all told in a writing style that chronicles every facet of each installment. His writing always makes certain that the reader is actually there, feeling what he felt in recalling the moment.

The authors that I most enjoy are those who have lived what they write. In that way, they don't write about something, but instead recall something worth sharing. Not every author can paint a page with recollections, and then, along comes Dorsey, and the page comes to life. You hear the contagious laughter of Lefty Kreh, or the familiar voice of Tom Brokaw. The piercing wit of Jimmy Kimmel or see, through Dorsey's words, the forming of glaciers, Caribbean sunrises, fly line loops unrolling, the smell of low tide or the curling smoke of campfires.

Clearly coming through the words of every chapter is Dorsey's appreciation of being a Dad and husband...his life afield not having left his family behind.

Two things impress me greatly about *Casting Call*. The collection tees up the opportunity for Dorsey to share his obvious abilities as a wordsmith (I await his first novel). His writing actually features the folks whose influences produced the adventures he portrays. He shares these folks with us in ways that make them our sidekicks, our mentors, our family.

Many outdoor scribes have caught billfish on flies, killed 180-inch whitetails, shot triples on a covey rise and they can clearly picture the events...Dorsey offers so much more. He also saw and describes the eagle that was watching that covey before it broke, the grapevine that the buck was nibbling before the report and the hypnotic rhythm of teasers trolled across the glistening dome of the Pacific.

In each chapter, Chris gives you the gift of the experience, which is not the photo of the fish, but all of the elements and relationships that caused the shutter to click in the first place.

Accept this book for the gift that it is.

— FP

Setting the Hook

With so much of our planet covered in liquid and with our bodies containing some 65 percent water, is it any wonder why we are drawn to rivers, lakes and oceans? Waters pose eternal questions that our innate curiosity feels compelled to try and answer: What's beneath the surface? What swims here? What are the fish telling us about our world? Will exploring the depths take us deeper into our own lives as we move about the globe to uncover the world's greatest angling?

That is the *why* of this book—if you hope to learn secrets that will create shortcuts to catching more fish, this book will likely disappoint you. On the other hand, if you are looking for a friend to share a journey to some of our planet's fishiest waters, step into the boat and let's go. We'll laugh and cry along the way and, in the end, we'll come out of the voyage changed fishers.

I didn't set out to write a book of fishing adventures, but rather a few decades of floating and wading the Earth—with some of the genre's greatest photographers and cinematographers—created an experience that, it seemed to me, was a worthy addition to the library of enduring titles that have blessed our tribe since Izaak Walton. Simply, this book is what happens when child-like curiosity is spiked with wanderlust and opportunity . . . and a team of the most talented eyes and minds to ever peer through a lens or a viewfinder.

Celebrating our planet's greatest fly angling by combining writing, photography and video became a mission to stimulate our emotions and create a sensory gift unique to the genre. That is, painting with words, light and sounds was a combination that hadn't been attempted so, given the riches of our expansive library, it was time.

Between tens of thousands of still photographs and an equal number of hours of video—married with a desire to paint a portrait of the fish and their homes that lure our kind to far corners of the globe—*Casting Call* is an invitation of sorts to write your own story and to share it with others who share this endearing way of life. It's for people who are drawn by exploration and adventure and who want to connect with one another through story.

Inside these pages and on the accompanying film, you will meet people like yourself, people you'll want to call your friend. You'll feel the wonder of meeting new waters and experiencing the awe of greeting a fish at the end of the line. When you fall in love with a flat, a river or a lake, it's impossible not to forever care about such places, for they become a part of you. If you listen, they will speak to you through the currents of time . . . sometimes telling you that they are in trouble and in need of help. When we set a hook, we are connected to more than a fish, but rather to our role as river keepers and guardians. This book holds up a mirror at times asking, *what do you see?* And, *what would you do . . . what is your role in writing the future?*

For many of us, the journey is about family: sons, daughters or perhaps *brothers* of sorts with whom we share the same spirit if not blood relations. Too, fishing is forever about connections—to each other, to places and to moments in time that live as long as we do. You'll find that in this book as well, maybe echoes of your own truth about waters and kinship, reminders that what we catch isn't nearly as important as what we keep . . . in our hearts and minds.

Join me around the next bend and let's explore beyond the horizon. Life will be all the better for it.

CHRIS DORSEY • Denver, Colorado

ABOUT THE AUTHOR

Chris Dorsey is among the world's most widely traveled sportsmen. He has fished and hunted on five continents, and has served in board leadership and advisory roles of numerous conservation and sporting advocacy organizations. He's a member of the Outdoor Legends Hall of Fame and is a recipient of the **Ray Scott Trailblazer Award** as well as the Curt Gowdy Memorial Award. He's a biologist, author of 11 books on outdoor subjects, is a past editor-in-chief of *Sports Afield* and *Ducks Unlimited* magazines. His work has appeared in most of the outdoor magazines in the English-speaking world as well as in *National Geographic, Newsweek, Forbes, The Wall Street Journal* and the *Robb Report.*

Dorsey has been called the "brand father" of outdoor television for having produced more than 2,000 episodes across 56 series with the largest brands in the outdoors. He's also hosted nearly 400 episodes and has fished freshwater and saltwater across the globe from Africa to Alaska and from South America to the South Pacific. His television productions are seen across the world and on a wide variety of U.S. mainstream cable and broadcast networks including ABC, Discovery Channel, HGTV, WGN America, DIY, Travel Channel, History Channel, National Geographic, Nat Geo Wild, Outdoor Channel, Animal Planet, Oxygen and others.

Whether through his countless television productions or the written word, Dorsey is relentless in celebrating and introducing the conservation and intrinsic values of the outdoor lifestyle to mainstream America. A nation that has no understanding of the role of sportsmen in building the foundation of conservation, he believes, cannot be counted on to advocate for its continued existence.

Dorsey holds degrees in English and Natural Resource Management from the University of Wisconsin-Stevens Point, and splits time with his family between Denver and Brays Island, South Carolina.

Contributing Photographers

John MacGillivray

Dusan Smetana

Marcos Furer

Francois Botha

R. Valentine Atkinson

Todd & Brad Reed

Designed by:

David Kirby,

Creative Connection

So many incredible
angling destinations...
so little time.

You say I'm a compulsive fishing freak like it's a bad thing. —Author Unknown

1 ▷ ▷ ▷

A good angler must not only bring an inquiring, searching, observing wit, but he must bring a large measure of hope.... —Izaak Walton

ICE OUT

Endless days amid the planet's richest fisheries

The invitation of an Alaskan river at the peak of the salmon run is as irresistible to an angler as a hopper is to a hungry brown in September.

Guide Ryan Burge and Heather Oberholtzer admire
one of Crystal Creek's legendary rainbows—
the heavyweights of the species. They possess
extraordinary fighting abilities, drawing
anglers from across the globe.

A Crystal Ball

Where The Rainbows Grow As Big As The Salmon

Bristol Bay is a place where fishermen with fat wallets go every year. For anglers of lesser means, it's a place that must be fished at least once before you die. For trout bums, it's where you go to work—if you're lucky.

Of the world's trout and salmon fisheries, none hold a fly rod to Bristol Bay. It sits at the eastern most arm of the Bering Sea in southwest Alaska and is 250 miles long and 180 miles wide at its mouth. Several of the world's greatest salmon rivers feed the bay, natal waters for millions of a range of different species that return to spawn each year. A few of the hallowed salmon superhighways include the Nushagak, Togiak, Ugashik, Naknek: all part of Mother Nature's vast nursery sustaining a complex and interconnected ecosystem that is as dependent on the seasonal movements of salmon as the Serengeti is the flow of wildebeest.

Bristol Bay supports all five species of Pacific salmon—sockeye, Chinook, coho, chum and pink—along with more than 20 other species of fish, 190 varieties of birds and 40 land animals that all rely on this rich landscape for critical parts of their life cycles. The Bristol Bay watershed produces nearly half of all the sockeye salmon in the world, generating $1.5 billion and supporting some 20,000 jobs annually. It is a natural protein factory the likes of which is unmatched anywhere in the world, and there's little doubt that its value was hardly contemplated when the U.S. purchased the territory from Russia in 1867. A toast to Mr. Seward, please.

Given the richness of this fishery, scores of premium lodges have been built throughout Bristol Bay to cater to anglers from across the globe who are looking to mine for the memories this piece of the planet so often delivers. Starting in June and July, king, sockeye and chum salmon all move into the

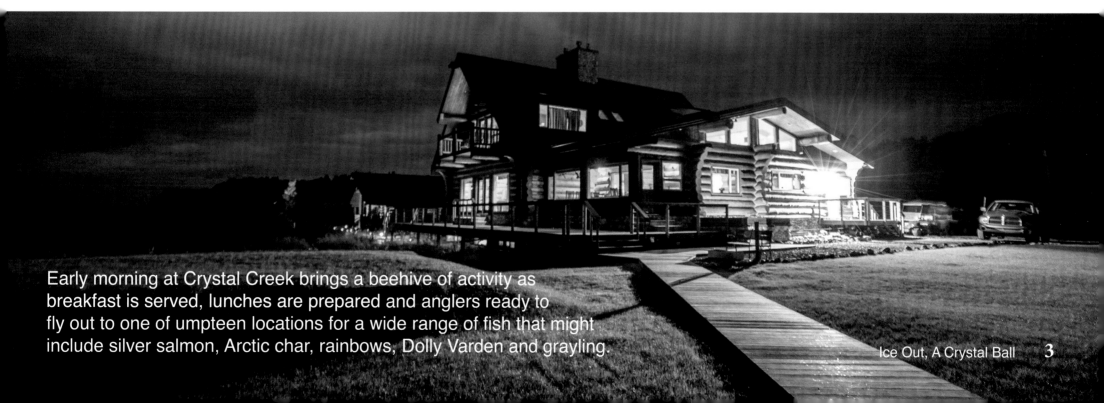

Early morning at Crystal Creek brings a beehive of activity as breakfast is served, lunches are prepared and anglers ready to fly out to one of umpteen locations for a wide range of fish that might include silver salmon, Arctic char, rainbows, Dolly Varden and grayling.

watershed. From August through September it's silver and humpback season. These fish migrations provide a three to four month working window for most lodges, each week offering a mixed menu of salmon species as well as local rainbows—the biggest in the world—char, grayling and Dolly Varden.

Joining me is Guido Rahr of the Wild Salmon Center, an Oregon-based group working to save ecosystems around the Pacific Rim that are vital to salmon and steelhead. Our home base for four days of fishing and exploration is none other than Crystal Creek Lodge, a Michelin-level destination amid the many fabled lodges found in and around Bristol Bay. It's located outside of King Salmon and is run by Dan Michels, a veteran of the premium sporting travel business that I first met many years earlier when he and his wife ran Buckeye Plantation in Georgia, one of those top-of-the-food-chain quail hunting venues visited by the same kind of folks booking in to Crystal Creek, just during different seasons of the year.

After a short ride in one of Crystal Creek's immaculately restored DeHavilland Beaver float planes, we are standing knee deep in the River Why, which is a code name for a small, trout-rich tributary that feeds into Lake Iliamna, the largest body of fresh water in all of Alaska. In addition to its sea-like size, the lake is so clean that you can drink directly from its waters, an unimaginable reservoir of purity. It is emblematic of a state that wears the moniker of "Last Frontier" like no other place could, pristine and largely untrammeled by the hand of man . . . for now.

The lake also is home to salmon-sized rainbow trout, the beasts that migrate out of Iliamna's waters each autumn to gorge themselves on salmon roe that turn these tributaries orange as the fish spawn and die. In the process, they release their nutrients and feed an entire ecosystem from the giant brown bears to the wolves to eagles and foxes and all manner of species in between—even the trees depend on the nutrient load carried upstream by the salmon. These arteries of fish are the basis of a remarkable natural story, one where the interdependence of species and habitat is intricate. Remove any one piece of the food chain here—especially the salmon—and this ancient natural theater becomes a house of cards.

Guido Rahr of the Wild Salmon Center and I are all smiles with a double hook-up inside Katmai National Park, an angler's paradise rich with salmon, trout and an ever-present gallery of giant brown bears.

Fishermen are the only children I know who can celebrate Christmas every day all summer long....
—Robert Traver

Guide Ryan Burge looks on as the author releases one of several 30-inch rainbows caught on the waters of the Naknek River. These steelhead-like, lake-dwelling rainbows move into the river during the salmon spawn to feast on the abundance of roe and protest mightily when their gorging is interrupted with a hook-set.

A released trout is like a wonderful dream you can have again and again.
—Harry Middleton

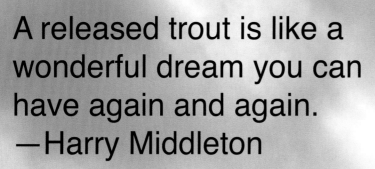

As I settle in and take my first cast, it's hit by a 25-inch rainbow that looks like some kind of laboratory hybrid, its hulking form super stuffed by the ridiculous abundance of sockeye eggs. The strength of these fish is legendary; they seem hell-bent on winning an egg-eating contest, as if they will soon join the bears in hibernation for the winter and must gain weight while the feeding is good.

"Try the seam just a little farther out," says guide Ryan Friel, as if he knows a secret that the river is about to share with me.

My cast hits the seam as instructed and a couple of seconds later I hook into a silver salmon, a brute of a fighter that takes me upriver as though he's reeling me in instead of the other way around. Then, suddenly, the beast jumps and transforms into a rainbow—a 30-inch-plus 'bow, the kind that are legend in these parts. Three more jumps later and he pops off, discarding my offering like a bucking bull throws a rider.

"Son of a . . . I thought that was a salmon," I say in disheartened disgust at having whiffed on a chance to stick one of the area's rainbow warriors, a leopard-printed beast that becomes addictive for fishermen once they experience the narcotic of the tug of a 30-incher. Instead, my line dangles in the water like the punchline to a bad joke—one that's on me.

One truth about fishing Alaska, however, is that redemption is never more than a cast away. A haul and a half later and a couple of mends and wouldn't ya know it I have a tiger, err, leopard 'bow by the tail—and it doesn't like it. The 27-inch fish spends more time airborne than in the water, leaping as if auditioning for the part of Atlantic salmon in this seasonal piscatorial play.

Between casts I'm able to catch up with Rahr who has been on the front lines working to save this unique ecosystem from a proposed copper and gold mine at the headwaters of Bristol Bay. Plans to develop Pebble Mine have sent ripples throughout the conservation and sporting community unifying sportsmen, manufacturers and environmental organizations like few other issues of the last half century.

"With incredible numbers of rivers and spring creeks feeding into Bristol Bay, salmon drive a wealth of nutrients up these systems as they migrate and it creates a perfect soup of biological productivity," says Rahr with a passion building in a crescendo as he describes the magic of the place.

We catch too many fish to worry about counting and head back to our Beaver that is parked on the edge of the lake, about a 500-yard walk from our secluded waters. Day one is just as I remember Bristol Bay, forever delivering on the promise of tight lines, one after another. As the throaty Beaver returns to the lodge, we get a bird's eye view of the surrounding waters and the landscape that Michels fell in love with when he first arrived more than a decade earlier.

Inside the spacious lodge appointed with comfortable furniture and all manner of Alaska native art and artifacts.

Crystal Creek is the kind of lodge you would conjure if someone you were with started speaking about Alaskan sport fishing. In addition to its dramatic, old-growth log construction with high beams and stunning views, it's perfectly positioned to offer a wide variety of Bristol Bay's best angling from several species of salmon to giant trout to Dolly Varden and char. A trio of De Havilland Beavers that appear newly minted, warm up each morning to transport guests to the far corners of the concession depending on daily fish movements and angling desires. Then there is the food: a Michelin experience served daily, using locally grown, caught and sourced ingredients. Arrive here and you have landed atop the angler's food chain.

The salmon are far more than protein providers, however, as they also serve as what biologists like to refer to as keystone species, canaries in the proverbial coal mine. As goes the salmon, so goes the rivers and the oceans. And, ultimately, us. Lose Bristol Bay and its salmon and there's no turning back the clock, for it would be yet another nail in the coffin of our planet, seemingly moving us ever closer to an ecological doomsday. Without the salmon these rivers would be little more than sterile drainages, for the fish are to coastal Alaska what the great caribou migrations are to the tundra, annual gifts of life to the entire ecosystem.

"The salmon provide massive pulses of marine nutrients gathered in the ocean and brought into the ecosystem as they migrate to spawn and die," says Rahr, distilling the essence of the fish and their environment.

The next day we board a Beaver with Michels in the cockpit. Our destination is the famed Brooks Falls, the iconic bear playground where behemoth browns sit like Labradors waiting for treats of salmon to jump upstream and into their jaws. It's the postcard view of the state celebrated in every Alaskan travel campaign. Funny how no one ever turns a picture of an open-pit mine into a postcard. Perhaps they should with a revised slogan: *Visit Alaska—It's the Pits.* Nothing like a dose of visual reality to bring sobriety to the situation.

At first, fishing amid the bears seems a risky proposition, the world's largest land carnivores with their trash-can-sized heads just 50 or 60 yards away. As I hook into my umpteenth 25-inch, super-charged rainbow, I watch a trio of brown bears on the other side of the river as they take notice of the splashing, triggering a Pavlovian response from the 1,500-pound carnivores. These are fish bears, growing three times the size of their interior grizzly cousins who do not have the benefit of the protein-rich salmon on which to gorge themselves. Then the three bears—papa, mamma and baby—ignore the trout and return their focus to the massive school of salmon under their noses.

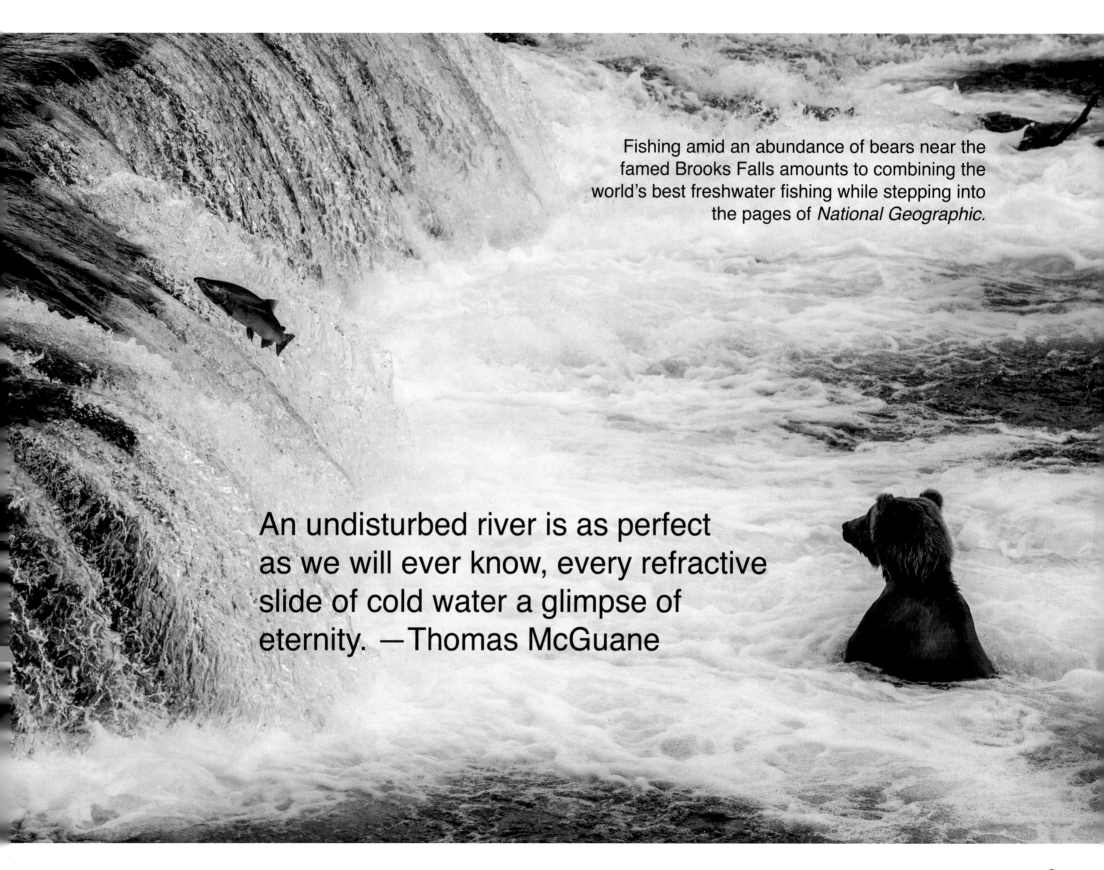

Fishing amid an abundance of bears near the famed Brooks Falls amounts to combining the world's best freshwater fishing while stepping into the pages of *National Geographic.*

An undisturbed river is as perfect as we will ever know, every refractive slide of cold water a glimpse of eternity. —Thomas McGuane

The Kvichak is, simply, one of the freshwater fishing wonders of the world, brimming with salmon and trout. It's also where the proposed Pebble Mine could be built, putting the head waters of Bristol Bay—the world's richest salmon fishery—at grave risk. The prospect of the mine lingers like a cancer on this land with conservationists occasionally beating the mine into remission . . . yet a cure remains elusive.

"These rainbows are a special breed," says guide Ryan Burge, "they're hotter than you've ever seen other rainbows."

Despite fish roe lining the bottom of these rivers, salmon egg beads are exceptionally effective at catching the big 'bows. This isn't a dry-fly purist's experience! Rather, is a daily tug of war with the brutes of Alaska. You come here to scrap, so save the technical finessing for smaller streams to the south.

As Rahr fights a fish pushing 30 inches, glancing over his shoulder to take inventory of the bears in the vicinity, he marvels at the health of this fishery.

"It used to be like this up and down the coast of the Pacific Northwest," he says. "Now we're spending hundreds of millions of dollars to try and bring back what once was. Here we can preserve what is—a far more cost-effective approach."

The headwaters of the Nushigak and Kvichak—our next venue of the trip—is where the proposed Pebble Mine would be located. When copper and gold are mined, the remaining tailings sometimes leach toxins into the watershed. Moreover, this is one of the most tectonically active zones in all the world, so expecting an earthen dam to hold back toxic waste water is a fool's errand. There's little hope that such a structure will last long term. Alaska experiences upwards of 10,000 earthquakes each year, more than 10 percent of the annual global total. Thus, there's a high probability that the poisons will eventually wind up in these pristine rivers, killing the salmon and everything that depends on it—likely forever.

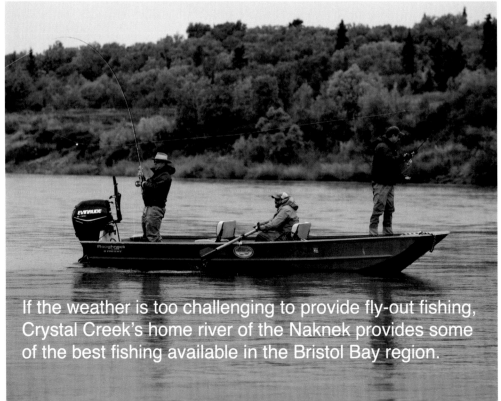

If the weather is too challenging to provide fly-out fishing, Crystal Creek's home river of the Naknek provides some of the best fishing available in the Bristol Bay region.

The question, then, becomes is it worth the risk? Can copper and gold be mined elsewhere that doesn't come with the potential of long-term devastation? If so, wouldn't it be wise to exploit those reserves before putting the world's richest salmon fishery at risk for what is a finite resource? What will we tell our kids: I wish you could have seen Bristol Bay when it was still amazing? All these questions hang in the air as we continue fishing, the magic of the experience making the prospect of the mine all the more unbelievable, surreal actually.

Just then, Rahr hooks into a trout that thinks it's a porpoise, the fish putting on an acrobatic display worthy of a Sea World warmup act, the massive fish launching missile like into the air before torpedoing to the depths of the river.

"If Mother Nature was to design the perfect trout stream, it would be the Kvichak," says Rahr. "It has a migration of ghost-like trout that come out of Iliamna and act like steelhead."

The last day breaks windy and rainy, conditions suitable only for bold pilots, not ones still among the living. What's there to do? Simply load a boat and head down river on the Naknek, the home river of the lodge. Within minutes, we are landing what seem, for all intents and purposes, to be steelhead. These are 30-inch rainbows that have grown humongous in the lake but can't resist the abundance of salmon eggs in the Naknek where they feed and grow even larger.

"There's nothing like the productivity of Bristol Bay. It is simply one of the most miraculous occurrences in nature," says Rahr. And the only way to insure something that's priceless is to protect it.

Because there's no replacing it. ●

Rahr, an Oregon resident, spends plenty of time in the Pacific Northwest employing a spey rod for steelhead. Here, he uses the rod to great effect on the broad waters of the Naknek.

What to Bring

Rods: Nine-foot 8-weight rod works for trout, char, Dolly Varden and most salmon. Kings require 10- to 12-weight

Reels: Good drag and lots of backing

Lines: Floating line for most, extra spool with sinking line helps

Flies: Wet flies imitating salmon eggs

Other Essential Gear: Waders, rain gear

Don't Forget to Pack: Video camera and cables to watch your footage each evening

Guide Ryan Friel, Rahr, Dorsey and Burge take a moment to memorialize one of the greatest fishing days of any life in the wild theater of Katmai National Park. Experience such breathtaking fishing and it's no wonder an angler will fight with all his might to protect such places, for their value is measured in memories that are irreplaceable.

Even when I do get so feeble that I cannot wade a stream, I shall have the blessed memories with me until the end. —Ray Bergman

I hold proof of the Naknek's fishing productivity, yet another rainbow stretching the 30-inch mark. As much as the great bears might be the poster creatures of Alaska, it is the fishery that is everything to The Last Frontier.

Just how fresh are these tracks? Just how hungry is the bear? Salmon-gorged brown bears pose little risk to anglers, for chewing through a pair of Simms waders is too much trouble when salmon are choking the rivers everywhere.

At the Crystal Creek dock, de Haviland Beavers become passports to adventure that are to the skies of Alaska what the Lund boat is to the state's waters. If transportation is needed to reach heaven, one or the other devices will most likely be used.

Every river has its own quality;
and it is part of wisdom to know
and love as many as you can.
—Henry Van Dyke

A sunset view from Crystal Creek brings the hope of good flying weather tomorrow . . . what to do? Silvers? Maybe char? What about Katmai? Such are the dilemmas facing visitors to this stretch of Bristol Bay.

Katmai brown bears grow to upwards of 1,500 pounds. While genetically the same as an interior grizzly, their protein-rich diet of salmon allows them to grow to three times the size of their grizzly cousins.

A happy wife is a happy life and nothing makes Amy smile like the end to a hard fight with a king salmon. Bristol Bay Lodge was one of the region's original destinations and is located amid some of the state's—hell, the *world's*—greatest freshwater fishing.

An Alaskan Original

There Are A Lot Of Places To Catch Salmon And Trout...

Just None Rivaling Bristol Bay

've never been much for sequels. That's especially true when it comes to fishing lodges. Great destinations start with the best waters and there's only so much of that. The birth of a fishing lodge usually goes something like this: A competent, adventurous angler prospects an area known to produce epic fishing, the kind that would attract other anglers to want to come visit. He then takes inventory of the best fishing in all the available waters. The next step is building a place in the midst of those prime waters before hanging a shingle.

Then come the sequels. Sometimes the thread count of the sheets they use on their beds or the vintage of the wines that they serve are better than the original, but the first lodge will always have the best fish and fishing. A great meal can be had in any city in America. Not so fishing. When it comes to lodges, beware imitations.

When it comes to Alaskan originals, then, Bristol Bay Lodge was one of the early fly fishermen's playgrounds built in the heart of the best salmon and trout angling on Earth. The lodge was constructed in 1972 by Ron and Maggie McMillan and many a fly-fishing soul has come to know Alaskan fishing through this portal to the state's captivating wilds. One of those free spirits was Steve Laurent, the guide turned owner-operator of the place, now going on 30 years.

My introduction to these waters was a dubious affair, for I was sitting in one of the lodge's remote out camps when word came over the radio of that fateful September 11th morning in New York and Washington D.C.. I was sharing the trip with old boss Matt Connolly, the long-time head of Ducks Unlimited. At the time, we didn't know what had happened and neither of us had a satellite phone in camp to reach family or friends for more clarity.

Matt Connolly channels his inner osprey as he searches for giant rainbows on the famed Togiak River.

Amy subdues yet another king fresh from the sea and that seems to revel in torture-testing her fly rod.

The radio report from base camp spoke only of a "disturbance" in New York and that a plane had flown into one of the World Trade Towers. Our assumption was that it was a small plane, undoubtedly the result of pilot error or perhaps a traumatic health issue. The news seemed peculiar but not monumental. It did, however, beg the question why would they even inform us of such trivial matters at a time when there were fish to be caught? It wasn't until we left the Alaskan bush and were able to absorb the constant media coverage that we realized September 12th began a new epoch on Earth.

Fifteen years later, Connolly and I decide to return to these waters, to celebrate that while the world may have changed that fateful day, life still goes on . . . salmon continue migrating and anglers still fret over how many they'll hook. Alaska remains the altogether intoxicating destination it's always been for sportsmen and we refuse to allow the work of a few of the world's bad actors to disrupt that.

The first morning we find ourselves anchored in a channel with a vein of silver salmon visible through crystalline waters to our left. The chrome fish are fresh from the sea where they've been dodging all manner of predators from seals and sea lions to sharks and orcas. These are the genetically honed survivors of the species and they are always ready to fight to the death. A hooked salmon doesn't know of catch and release and forever errors on the side of caution by using all of its strength to try and earn its freedom.

I don't even finish my first mend before one of the torpedoes is ripping bus-length sections of line as my Helios becomes a fish-finding diving rod of sorts. In the instant the salmon makes its first jump there is a slow motion moment in my mind's eye that takes me back 15 years, as if this is a continuation of the last silver I caught all those years ago. Then I wonder why the hell it's been so long since I've been back, for there hasn't been much on my September calendars any more inviting than Alaskan salmon and trout fishing. Maybe once you fish here, however, a piece of you never really leaves, for Alaska like any other seductress doesn't let you forget her easily.

"Bristol Bay Lodge is in the prime center of being within striking distance of so many different angling experiences that are incredible," says Connolly, a man who looks upon his passport as something of a universal fishing license, having traveled to many of our planet's prime angling offerings.

Since both of us have a penchant for the mega rainbows of Alaska, we strike off to the Agulapak, one of the best trout waters in this stretch of Bristol Bay. The skies are clear, there's no wind, and a general sense of euphoria permeates the mood as we boat our way to the start of a drift famous for producing an abundance of hard-fighting fish. Guide Blake Enyart, a tall thin shad of a man who sometimes takes on the human form of an osprey, is weaving us through the boulders and current, introducing us to the 'bows with whom he seems to be on a first name basis.

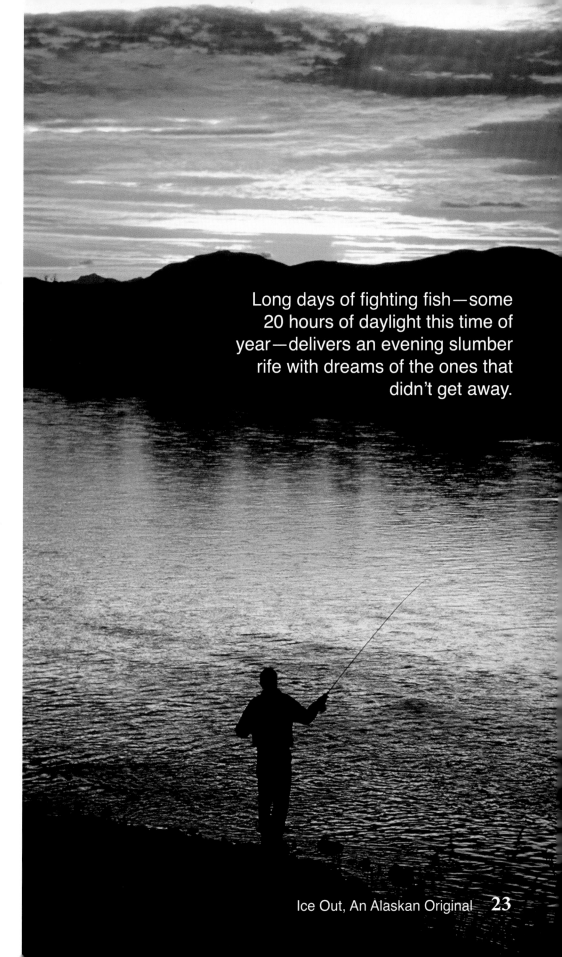

Long days of fighting fish—some 20 hours of daylight this time of year—delivers an evening slumber rife with dreams of the ones that didn't get away.

A few minutes in and my 6-weight suddenly takes the shape of a question mark as the first trout of the trip comes looking for a fight. Given the legendary strength of these fish, the questions are always: How big is this beast and will I get it to the boat? A few runs later and Enyart is scooping the 24-inch 'bow into his net, giving it no more deference than he might a creek chub. While a Montana angler will burn a lot of pixels on a 24-inch rainbow, in these parts it's considered a warm up, an appetizer for the main course of fish stretching past 27 and 28 inches. There's always a chance for a sacred 30-incher as well. Tell me size doesn't matter . . . with all forms of trout.

Once a rainbow reaches these dimensions, it seems something of a different species as the fight is more salmon or steelhead like. On our first foray to Bristol Bay, I had just landed one of the 30-inch legends in a small stream that Matt and I were fishing. Within minutes, Connolly hooked a fish that was larger, a ridiculous eye-popping generational hog. It's the kind that would be remembered by grandkids and great grandkids in school yards down the familial line.

"My great grandfather invented the atom bomb."

"Mine once ran for the game winning touchdown when Notre Dame won the national championship."

"That's nice, mine caught a 35-inch rainbow in Alaska 50 years ago."

"No way!" chimes the chorus.

I stood behind Connolly, watching the seminal moment play out. As the saying goes, I remember it like it was yesterday. Strangely, the guide seemed distracted, maybe thinking about a girlfriend who just dumped him from afar or the lodge hookup that was an upgrade from previous flings—who knows? What I do know is that Connolly brought in an epic rainbow: the largest of his life—hell, maybe anyone's life—to the pebbles of the bank and the guide nonchalantly walked to retrieve the net, picked it up and slowly ambled toward the fish. About the time he reached the leviathan, the fish made one last flop, popping the hook and slipping back to the depths of the creek, its dimensions never to be confirmed.

If it's giant rainbows you seek—and who doesn't?—follow the trail of spawning salmon as the trout will be near the heaviest concentration of eggs. The wide variety of waters—from broad rivers to intimate streams—are part of the charm of fishing in this stretch of Alaska. No matter the size of the water, giants can be found almost anywhere.

The dock at Bristol Bay Lodge is the launching pad for scores of daily fly-out adventures to some of the most prime waters in all of Alaska.

Create the life you want, then fish it. —Paul Quinnett

"Fudge," is all I could hear Matt utter.

Only he didn't say fudge. I looked at my shoes for most of the trip back, thankful Connolly didn't have a gun or knife on him or I'm convinced that I would have been witness to a murder. Presented with the evidence, however, there isn't a jury in Alaska that would have convicted him, a true case of justifiable homicide if ever there was one.

The best way to forget about such an instant—other than years of therapy and some measure of pharmaceuticals—is to create a memory that fills the void of what could have been. I've used the displacement memory method to rescue numerous such outings over a lifetime of fishing and hunting. In Connolly's case, it means heading to the Togiak to join Carter Simcoe for the last vestiges of the silver salmon run.

As the DeHavilland Beaver sets down, Simcoe greets us with the news that he's found a couple of pockets of new fish downriver. It was just what the shrink ordered.

Soon Connolly is engaged in hand-to-rod combat, trying desperately to subdue one of the silvers that has no intention of being shore lunch. Two jumps into Connolly's encounter, a silver nearly rips the rod from my hand. After two days of catching rainbows and Dolly Varden, the silvers have us recalibrating our grips in an electric, double hookup moment that feels like we are caught in some salmon vortex where we can't escape the endless tug of the fish.

We end the morning with elated exhaustion, like a football team that fought to the end and prevailed. The silvers tested our mettle but now it's time to enjoy an Alaskan spin on the shore lunch, and Simcoe is eager to showcase his culinary talents. Over the course of several days of fishing with multiple guides, it becomes clear that there is a bit of a competition brewing as to which one has the winning shore lunch recipe.

With a colorful mix of sautéed root vegetables and onions along with salmon covered in a light tempura coating, Simcoe delivers a performance worthy of a Michelin rating. We concur that neither of us has ever had better on any shoreline anywhere. There's nothing like turning a fish that was swimming an hour earlier into lunch to make you want to keep fishing.

Feeling like the over-stuffed bears of the river, we waddle our way back to the bank to continue casting for more silvers. Connolly hooks up again, suddenly holding a lightning rod as a brute of a silver porpoises downstream, apparently well aware of what happens to a salmon when Simcoe is around.

Every fishing water has its secrets . . .
And to yield up these mysteries, it must be
fished with more than hooks. —Zane Grey

The mixed menu of fishing opportunities in this
stretch of Bristol Bay are a guide's dealer's
choice, for the fishing opportunities are limited
only by the migrations and weather.

When I fish in wild Alaska, I sometimes wonder if it is fish I am really after. I venture here just to remind myself that such places still exist . . . then I hatch plans to spend more time in such environs in what has become my life's never-ending quest to escape civilization.

Guides in Alaska are often given a stretch of river to manage for the season, until the last of the runs wane or the fish move to other stretches of the Bristol Bay watershed through the course of their seasonal migrations. Fresh anglers are cycled in and out of the remote camps and for a season the river becomes something of a guide's possession. Thus, there's nothing but the movement of fish, bears, wolves and the currents of time to occupy a guide's mind for much of their wilderness stay. That, and apparently experimenting with new shore lunch concoctions.

In a season, a guide will discover whether he's comfortable in his own skin, for despite the fact that there is a rotation of visiting anglers, there is enough down time between shifts to get to know yourself with only the company of your own thoughts. For some, that provides solace and comfort in nature's womb. For others in constant need of societal stimulation, wilderness is a prison to be escaped.

It's clear Simcoe could stay here until either the salmon—or beer—run out. That's just the kind of guide with whom you want to fish, especially since the bush is a lousy place to have to cope with neurosis. Because of weather and fish

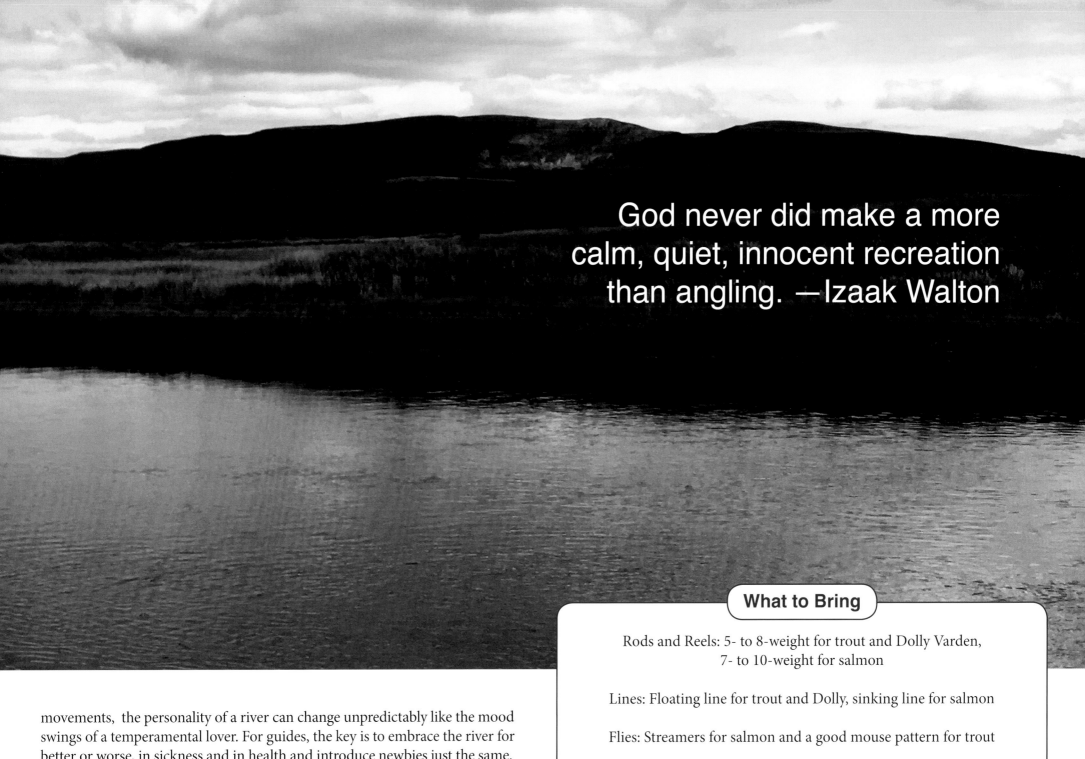

God never did make a more calm, quiet, innocent recreation than angling. —Izaak Walton

movements, the personality of a river can change unpredictably like the mood swings of a temperamental lover. For guides, the key is to embrace the river for better or worse, in sickness and in health and introduce newbies just the same.

For Laurent, living and working Bristol Bay Lodge for three decades, flying its bush planes and generally delivering angling dreams is all he's ever known. It's all he's ever wanted to know. In the process, he's created a place you simply don't want to leave. The kind of destination he can't leave, either. Some would say, it's even better than the original.

As much as it is pleasant to enjoy the comforts of a luxury Alaskan fishing lodge, it is the fly-out camps where the true flavor of the state's wilderness—with the sounds of wolf howls at night and eagle fights by day—takes hold in your psyche.

Connolly prepares to do battle with yet another feisty rainbow. While the salmon are often the original lure for visiting anglers, once you experience the tiger-by-the-tail fight of an Alaskan 'bow, you'll forever be in search of more. Catching and fighting these wickedly robust fish becomes a piscatorial narcotic of sorts.

Fishing is a condition of mind wherein one cannot possibly have a bad time. —Zane Grey

An easy boat ride from Bristol Bay Lodge and I'm standing knee deep in opportunities for rainbows and Dolly Varden. Can't fly because of the weather? No problem.

Connolly has a spring in his step after being delivered by float plane to one of several remote camps scattered throughout Bristol Bay Lodge's vast fishing territory.

Fishing makes us less the hostages
to the horrors of making a living . . .
It is a time warp we may step into for
a little peace. —Jim Harrison

The stream, which had been dull
and sullen all day long, broke into a
cheerful smile. —Charles Dickens

Rowswell hoists another 20-pound pike from the shallows after I set the hook on a red and white flesh fly that proved irresistible to the Saskatchewan pike. Sight-casting to log-sized pike after ice out might be the continent's most memorable freshwater fly-fishing experience.

Pike On The Fly

When Ice-Out Comes To The North Country, Beware The Lord Of The Ambush

As the pontoons of the twin-engine Otter break the surface tension of a nameless Saskatchewan lake, a nearly imperceptible touch-down only made obvious by the spray of water off the floats, it triggers a kind of endorphin in my blood. I become a child once more. It's as if school's out for the summer and we're going camping at a metaphoric lake that represents every magical outdoor experience of my life.

I turn to my twin sons Luke and Nate, looking for a glimmer of what I felt as a kid caught up in the wonderment of a much more modest fishing and camping adventure. What is the anticipation they're feeling and what will this remote piece of Canada mean to them in a week when we leave? The expedition is part of my eternal quest to build shared passions and memories with my sons, a love of a way of life that has meant so much to me.

I go into the mission with trepidation—a heavy hand will surely turn them away and such a result would be the greatest disappointment of my life. No pressure. *I must go softly, deliberate yet patient in letting them process this world,* I think to myself. *It's the only way it'll become their own.* As we leave the plane, I surrender to the truth that only a divine hand will bind us in this love of all things wild. It's best if I simply make the introduction and get out of the way. *Please, Lord, make it so . . . Amen.*

I can't think of a better person to help baptize the boys into the north country than Kevin Rowswell, an outfitter friend with whom I have been hunting and fishing on and off for more than two decades. Like many Canadians I have known, he's an affable sort whose dry humor improves proportionally with the addition of Labatt's or Crown Royal, at least it seems that way as I try and keep pace. I first met him as he shared the magic of the waterfowl and Hungarian partridge hunting near his Cut Knife, Saskatchewan, home. Given that we possess the same love of the Canadian countryside and all that it offers the hunter-angler, we've stayed in touch since.

Fish fry, anyone? Son Luke only needed 15 minutes to return with a stringer of walleyes for lunch.

There comes a time in every man's life when he is either going to go fishing or do something worse. —Havilah Babcock

When I first joined him at his pike and walleye fly-in camp in the far north of the province, I marveled at the sheer plethora of hungry pike, every-other-cast walleye and abundant lake trout. Every Midwestern pike and walleye angler looks upon the Canadian northland as a fishing utopia, the kind of place any bumpkin can fill a stringer. It's not that simple, however. In order to find such waters you need to go beyond the reach of the numerous tribes that are especially adept at separating a lake from its walleye. It's an ancient gift . . . now aided and abetted by modern equipment.

At the height of the fish wars between the tribes in Wisconsin and the state's 1.5 million sport anglers, I once saw a bumper sticker showing a spear with the phrase, "Flambeau Fly Rod," created after a court ruling that allowed the Flambeau Band to spear muskie and pike in the spawn. It's a practice that will make the angels weep, no matter your God. Pictures of log-sized muskies—the dream of catching such a fish lured Chicago anglers in droves to northern Wisconsin each year where they fed an entire regional economy—were published in Milwaukee newspapers, further enraging sport fishermen. For the tribes, it was the best payback they could conjure. That is, until they opened casinos and essentially began taxing the white man, first plying him with alcohol to grease the fleecing, amounting to a century's old turnabout.

We have come to Canada to experience the magic of the northland's wilderness and to avail ourselves of some of the greatest freshwater angling in the world, far from the influence of man—red or white. In the process, perhaps my sons will become better men for having spent time with the Rowswells and maybe we will become closer as a family, a "by-catch" we'd welcome. It's tough to put such value on a stringer, but as Ben Franklin once wrote, "Lost time is never found again."

Rowswell's homemade motorized wheelbarrow makes a portage to a hidden lake brimming with walleye and pike a breeze.

My wife Amy, a daddy's girl who grew up catching whatever swam in the ponds near their home in southern Virginia, joins us as well, sharing her piscatorial DNA with our sons in whom the fishing force appears strong.

Luke and I join Kevin in one boat and Amy and Nate are guided by Kevin's thirty-something son, Jordan.

In the north country, planes are De-Havillands and boats are Lund's as surely as the fish are pike and walleye. We strike off to wind our way through the innumerable pools connected by a vast river system that stretches hundreds of miles, a limitless fishery home to no humans other than us. Luke is armed with a spin rod and a red Dardevle, the two inventions that have occupied more boys for longer than even the one-eyed Wooly Bugger. The desire of man to catch a fish and the angst at not being able to do so must surely be among our species oldest emotions. That and the complete mystery surrounding the opposite sex.

Two casts into his inaugural Canadian angling adventure, Luke hooks an arm-length pike, not a monster but a welcomed offering from the fish gods, nonetheless. As a young kid—eight and nine years old—he would cast for hours in ponds near our home in Colorado,

The savage take of a pike is the hallmark of this form of tug-of-war fishing. In Saskatchewan's far north, countless giant pike that have never seen a fly await your arrival. Land a 40-incher on an 8-weight and hold on tight for you will be part of an ancient rodeo.

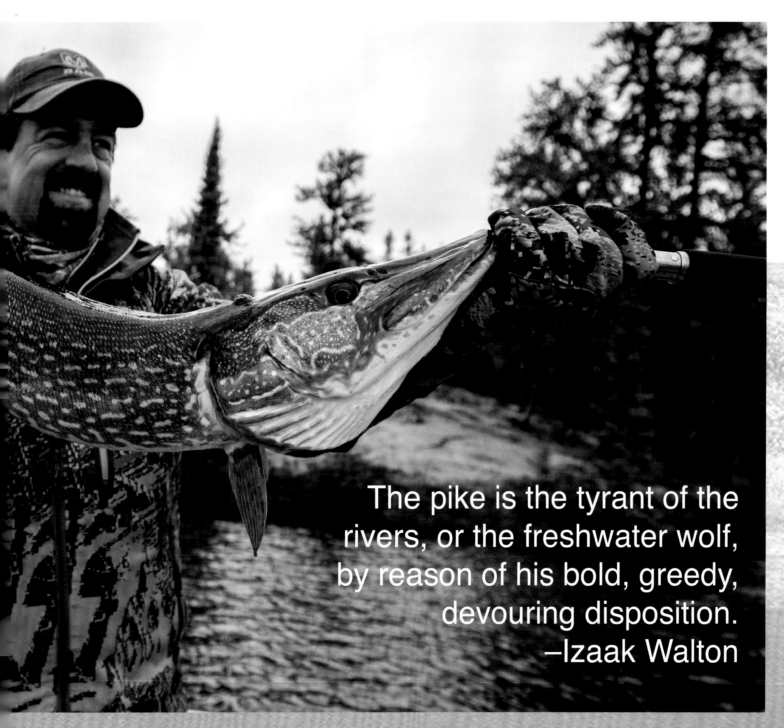

The pike is the tyrant of the rivers, or the freshwater wolf, by reason of his bold, greedy, devouring disposition.
—Izaak Walton

perfecting his technique to the point where he could flip a lure under an overhanging tree and hit a pie plate at 40 yards. His motivation? To catch a couple of eight-inch bass in an afternoon, as if to prove that these cow tanks did, indeed, have fish in them. Amy and I marveled at his persistence, knowing that our attention spans at that age would have drifted after but a few minutes.

As Kevin hoisted the pike, Luke had the look of someone recalibrating his expectations. *If I could catch a fish like this so quickly, just what am I in for this week?* his grin suggested. For Kevin, what could be better than seeing a kid who loves to fish greet one of his pike? Why, landing many, of course!

This Precambrian Shield as it is called, is a leftover gift from the glaciers of the last Ice Age, 10,000 years ago, for they carved and scraped innumerable lakes out of the granite. Then, as they retreated, they had the decency to fill the flowages with their meltwater. There's seemingly an even mix of terra and not-so-firma muskeg and lakes that are the hallmarks of the territory. This region became the planet's ultimate nursery for growing endless schools of vicious pike, walleye, lake trout and grayling. We're just here to check in on the stocks and make sure they're doing okay.

For a man to admit a distaste for fishing would be like denouncing mother-love or hating moonlight.
-John Steinbeck

After a morning of taming dozens of mid-sized pike, it's getting toward lunch, which means it's time to catch the main ingredient. Up here, that means walleye, which is Chipewyan for *delicious*. We have an hour before noon, plenty of time to catch enough fish to fry on the bank, like some kind of northland drive-through. It's seldom a question if you're going to catch fish here, it's just a matter of how many and what size. As a lifelong short-attention-span angler, it's the perfect prescription for an angling holiday.

Kevin fillets 10 fat walleye and soon the battered fillets are sizzling in hot oil on the banks of a lake with skies above as blue as saxophone music. It is an idyllic day in the North Country, and the combination of fish, fried potatoes and onions and baked beans might as well have been the private dining menu of the French Laundry. But I wouldn't trade it for such.

As we recline on the carpet of moss that covers much of the northwoods waiting for the walleye to finish cooking, a young black bear gets a whiff of the impromptu kitchen and ambles in to see about crashing the party. Despite six of us both sitting and standing around, he ambles to within 30 yards before Jordan grabs a shotgun and chases him off, the universal signal meaning *no soup for you.*

A boulder-strewn river is no problem for Rowswell's hovercraft that seems more spaceship than boat. The device delivers us to otherwise inaccessible pools where we take a break from fly casting to try our luck with spinning rods.

With a belly full of walleye, Nate and I go with Kevin to a large flat off the main flowage, it's the kind of shallow pool pike favor on sunny days to warm up after ice-out, which occurred just a couple of weeks earlier. The warmth helps activate their systems and recharges them to battle with anglers looking for a brawl. We have come to pick a fight, for the 20-pounders found in these parts are unquestionably some of the strongest fish in the world of freshwater fishing.

When I first landed here with Matt Connolly, some 13 years earlier, we discovered these waters and every 50 yards or so there seemed to be a log-sized pike sunning itself, a stunning aggregation of behemoths that only this part of the world produces with any kind of regularity. Sight casting to a 20-pound pike, pitching a flesh pattern past its nose and stripping it for all you're worth is the simple technique. As the fly zips past a fish, the brutes will coil and swipe the water with their tails, shooting them head-long into the fly like a cobra hits a rat. It's a wicked assault deserving of a police report.

What makes it all the more delicious is the fact that all of this is visible. Once you've watched the take and have hooked into a 50-inch northern, it's *you* that is hooked. It's one of the great sight-casting experiences found anywhere, for they are a prehistoric beast leftover from the Jurassic . . . probably possessing recombinant piscatorial *and* dino DNA. Look into the eyes of a pike and you will see the vacuous soul of an executioner. Their mantra is simple: seek and devour.

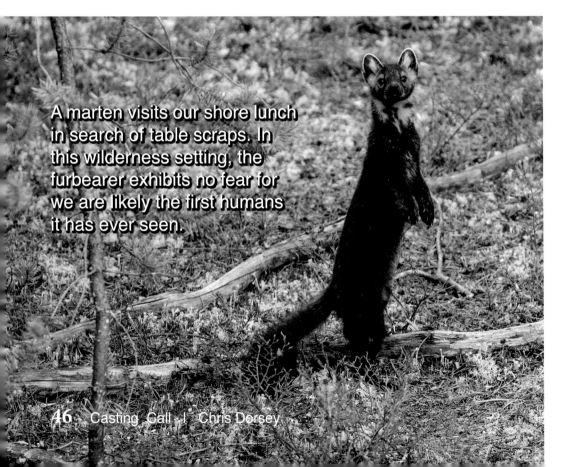

A marten visits our shore lunch in search of table scraps. In this wilderness setting, the furbearer exhibits no fear for we are likely the first humans it has ever seen.

Wolves and black bears are the apex predators of the region. This stretch of Saskatchewan is loaded with bears and it's not uncommon to see several each day wandering the shoreline as you fish for a mix of pike, walleye and lake trout.

Sometimes the fishing is so good that you just can't leave—at least not without making one last cast before boarding the float plane and returning to the world of concrete and lights.

Fishing consists of a series of misadventures interspersed by occasional moments of glory.
—Howard Marshall

Shortly after ice out, monster pike move into the shallows to warm themselves and kick-start their digestive system. Drop a 10-inch fly in front of a pike and you'll witness millions of years of predatory instinct take over as the fish cocks its tail and rockets into the fly in a vicious mugging.

It wouldn't be a north country fishing trip without a classic shore lunch of walleye, fried potatoes and beans . . . and don't forget the tartar sauce. Eating fish that was swimming an hour earlier delivers flavors never to be found in the frozen food section of your local grocery.

For Nate, who is a budding fly fisherman, a 25-yard cast to a pike in the bay brings his first sight-cast hookup, the fish making a couple of strong runs before Nate is able to subdue him. Now it's my turn. Kevin poles the Lund through the shallows as we take inventory of the available pike. Perhaps 20 minutes into the float, we spy a monster.

This is a fish well in excess of 20 pounds, so there's an electricity in the boat at the prospect of convincing the fish to eat my red and white flesh fly. I make three casts, stripping the fly at various angles in front of his nose. Nothing but rejection.

Then as we drift a bit closer—about 25 yards away—I can see one of the fish's eyes is milky, likely blind on that side. I make one more cast to the other side of the fish and it pounds the fly, unloading its magnum charge and making two 60-yard-plus runs before finally tapping out. Hoisting the 25-pound fish is *deja vu*, for the shallow bay delivers just as I remember it doing more than a decade ago.

It's impossible to know where the currents of time will take us, but for one week of our lives we fell in love with a place and a moment. We'll always have the memory of this land and its waters to share, and for twin 14-year-olds, the good Lord provided the fish and they took the bait, forever to be fisherman. Just as I hoped. Just as I prayed.

Hallelujah! 🌎

The hovercraft is to this stretch of remote Saskatchewan what the airboat is to the Everglades, for it delivers visitors to places seldom—if ever—seen by man. The contraption is a magic carpet of sorts that provides hidden adventures and memories that will endure as long as we do.

What to Bring

Rods and Reels: 8- or 9-weight for pike

Lines: Steel leader! Pike's teeth will make short work of most lines

Flies: Four to six inches in length, red/white and red/yellow patterns

Other Essential Gear: Protection from sun and rain

Don't Forget to Pack: A positive attitude to deal with the changing weather

There is certainly something in angling that tends to produce a gentleness of spirit, and a pure serenity of mind.
—Washington Irving

Wheeler River Lodge is one of Canada's most remote destinations and is located in the midst of hundreds of miles of connected lakes and rivers that would be impossible to explore by boat in many lifetimes—but it would be fun to try.

Occasionally we shared our waters with other of the region's anglers. I can't help but wonder what the eagles must think of our intrusion into their untrammeled wilderness.

Guide George Cromwell greets dawn on the Bow in time to catch the first hatch of the day.

All men are equal before trout.
—President Herbert Hoover

The Blue Ribbon Bow
Knee Deep In One Of Alberta's Great Fly Waters

I was minding my own business while sitting at one of Calgary's outdoor cafés one evening overlooking the Bow River when I noticed what looked like an overgrown firefly making its way to the river. I had a night to kill before heading to the tundra for an appointment with caribou. The river-bound bug turned out to be an angler using a lamp to guide his methodical approach to the stream, apparently part of a unique hatch this night.

In the hour that I sat mesmerized by the night angler, I could see him pull in what I counted to be six fish, the splashing water of the last vestiges of each fight flickering in the illumination of his headlamp. Witnessing such productive angling in an urban setting started my investigations into all things Bow River and trout fishing. Two years later, I returned.

The meandering river begins its journey in Banff National Park in the mountains outside of Calgary and continues its quiet trek through the city, seemingly unnoticed by visitors who are mostly drawn by civic attractions—except for the occasional pub-crawling caddisfly addict. There is a small, cult-like local group, however, who are keenly aware of the river and all it represents. It is an ecological marvel. These waters support a trout fishery that rivals some of the continent's best waters. Welcome to the blue-ribbon Bow, population: 2,500 trout per river mile.

The nutrient-rich waters downstream from Calgary sport the river's best trout populations. Though the river begins its journey in the Rockies west of the city, it is a sterile waterway until it reaches Calgary—where nutrients from municipal effluent turn the river into a trout factory, where streamsmiths hold their noses and live their greatest trouting fantasies. I've never much cared to eat trout, so how they proliferate isn't as interesting to me as the fact that they do. I, for one, am glad the river is *flush* with fish . . . and don't worry, the river aesthetic is quite inviting and you needn't be concerned with "mud minnows" floating past!

The trout here grow big and thick. And they don't bite a fly so much as they *hammer* it. I was innocently casting a nymph upstream of a small riffle when I saw my line lunging downstream faster than the current could have been taking it.

The slack in my line soon gave way to the trout, and my reel began to hiss as the brute pulled large bolts of line into the water. With nothing but a few strands of backing left on the reel, the fish tired enough for me to rewind a full third of my line, only to have him yank it back downstream in a last attempt to escape. The fish seemed well-versed at using the river's current to make it appear larger than it is, sort of like the fiction of a football program.

The exhausted fish flopped side to side in the clear current of the river during the last rounds of battle. As I cupped him in my hands, his tired eyes seem to suggest: *Kill me if you must, but first know that you won't enjoy it.*

I released the 20-inch linebacker of a rainbow back into the current. It is in that brief moment when an angler is eye-to-eye with a trout that the sport casts its spell. Holding the perfection of a trout with a pimple of a fly stuck to its lip, watching it glisten out of the water in a riot of colors is, in effect, a connection to another dimension of our planet—the secretive underworld of a stream.

The waters below Calgary deliver a steady diet of hefty and hard-fighting rainbows that didn't seem as finicky as some of the trout in the western U.S.

The lower Bow is a meandering prairie river with the endearing combination of low fishing pressure and plenty of hungry trout.

The Bow is reminiscent of many rivers of the western U.S. save for the relative lack of angling pressure.

For guide George Cromwell, the Bow River is both his office and a therapist. He has been plying these waters for a decade and, while his instruction is expert, it does not take a pro to land a trout here . . . I'm living proof of that. As we drift downriver, I begin landing 16- to 18-inch fish every 10 to 15 minutes or so, the river proving generous as it welcomes me to her abundance of trout.

The Bow starts as a rapidly moving mountain stream and becomes a gentle prairie river below Calgary. It's easy to be distracted by the dramatic, rocky bluffs that rim the bank in some stretches of its course. Ducks, geese, herons and even loons can be seen while testing the river for trout. The occasional pheasant cackles on one of the innumerable islands in the river's braided course before flying to adjacent fields to feed. Around every bend in the river is

A multi-day float with nightly campfires makes for a memorable way to experience this slice of Alberta, one of the great sporting provinces of Canada.

a unique vista, offering a different perspective to the land than the terrain you may have floated only moments before. Even if the fishing were slow—which it isn't—a float provides scenic diversions and a front-row seat to the inviting terrain. Add a couple of beers and it gets even better.

After setting up our first camp about 15 miles downstream from Calgary—a pup tent and bed rolls—Cromwell and I set out for our last casts in the magic twilight before nightfall. Ahead of me, a calm eddy began bubbling with trout rises. I fumble around trying to hurriedly replace my nymph with a terrestrial, a hopper to be specific. The trout are impatient and Cromwell is already netting and releasing a handsome rainbow before I even offer my first dry to the fish.

Rainbows in the 20-inch range are common on the Bow and some will stretch the 25-inch mark. No matter the size, however, the fish are skilled at leveraging the current to amplify their fight.

Fishing is a great deal like sex. When it's good, it's absolutely wonderful. And when it's bad, it's still pretty damn good.
—William Tapply

Constructing makeshift overnight camps near the river's most productive riffles is good living.

y hopper has scant little time to absorb any water before a rainbow smashes it, sending spray into the air like the strike of a Florida bass. I feel like a garden spider that has spun a web strong enough to catch a fly, but not one necessarily able to snare a powerful locust. I am, like the spider, hanging on to see if my line will endure long enough to subdue the fish. A sudden turn upstream, however, gives the trout just enough slack to shake free of my barbless hook. While the line held, the results are no different than had the leader snapped. It's always something . . . especially with the biggest fish.

It is the memories of these fish—the ones that escape—that preoccupies my thoughts as an angler. There are so many unanswered questions with lost fish: How big was it, really? What could I have done differently to keep him on the hook? How many other anglers had this fish escaped? The list is endless. If every question were answered, I guess, we'd have no reason to fish, for each cast begins an investigation to solve a river mystery where the clues are more about appreciating art than understanding science. To be sure, we are fishing for answers as much as we are fish, they're merely the reason for the journey and exploration. I have friends among the bamboo brigade who swear, after extended periods on the water, that they sometimes dream in trout. But they're the ones who tend to fish with roaches.

Cromwell hoists one last 'bow before heading off to start a fire and prepare dinner of grilled steaks.

Surrounding our secluded camp is a series of rocky ridges on both sides of the river, the canyon providing what feels like a private slice of Alberta trout magic. As night descends, the bluffs become an amphitheater for coyotes that engulf the canyon with their a cappella yodels. It is a primordial concert sending me off to an amniotic slumber in Mother Nature's womb.

The morning of the last day of the voyage breaks cold, as if we've been put on notice that Indian summer has given way to autumn. September's cool mornings bring the trout to the surface of calm eddies outside our makeshift camp, where we hope our Light Cahill and caddisfly facsimiles will seduce a brute from the depths. A couple of quick tease casts and I drop the caddis where I had seen a fish surface only a couple of heartbeats earlier. Then in a piscatorial sleight of hand, the fly vanishes from the surface as if someone spliced the film, removing the one second of the heist. A few minutes later, I'm saying hello to the 25-inch rainbow before releasing it back to its home pool.

Rods in the 5- to 7-weight class are ideal for fishing on the river. Going with a little stiffer rod helps when prairie winds kick up.

Limestone bluffs line much of the river and provide a dramatic setting in which to fish. One of the most endearing aspects of trout fishing is that they seldom live in ugly places.

While plenty of fish are caught from a boat, wading the river's many productive riffles is the classic way to fish the Bow.

There are plenty of hatches in late summer, so dry-fly purists will cotton to this river.

Later in the day, we return to our time-honored ritual of heaving weighted nymphs. Cromwell rigs a San Juan Worm dropper with a Brooks Yellow Stone nymph as the point fly. Out of the water the combination looks like a jackrabbit snare, but beneath the surface, its trout-attracting properties are undeniable.

Anglers use these patterns with considerable success on the river from late May through October. Even the winter months, however, don't deter the Bow's hardy angling aficionados. A January or February thaw—rare though they may be—will send fishermen out of the bars and back to the banks of the river for sorely needed cabin fever therapy.

While the Bow may never own the mystique of some of our continent's other celebrated trout waters, its lack of a public relations campaign provides anglers with a chance to beat the crowds common on other waters. These days, that might be the biggest draw of all. 🎣

What to Bring

Rods and Reels: 6-weight

Lines: Floating for dry flies, weight-forward for streamers and nymphs

Flies: Match the hatch . . . otherwise, Clouser minnows, leeches or a hopper with a dropper will always work.

Other Essential Gear: Lightweight rain jacket

Don't Forget to Pack: Camera—the scenery and wildlife are breathtaking

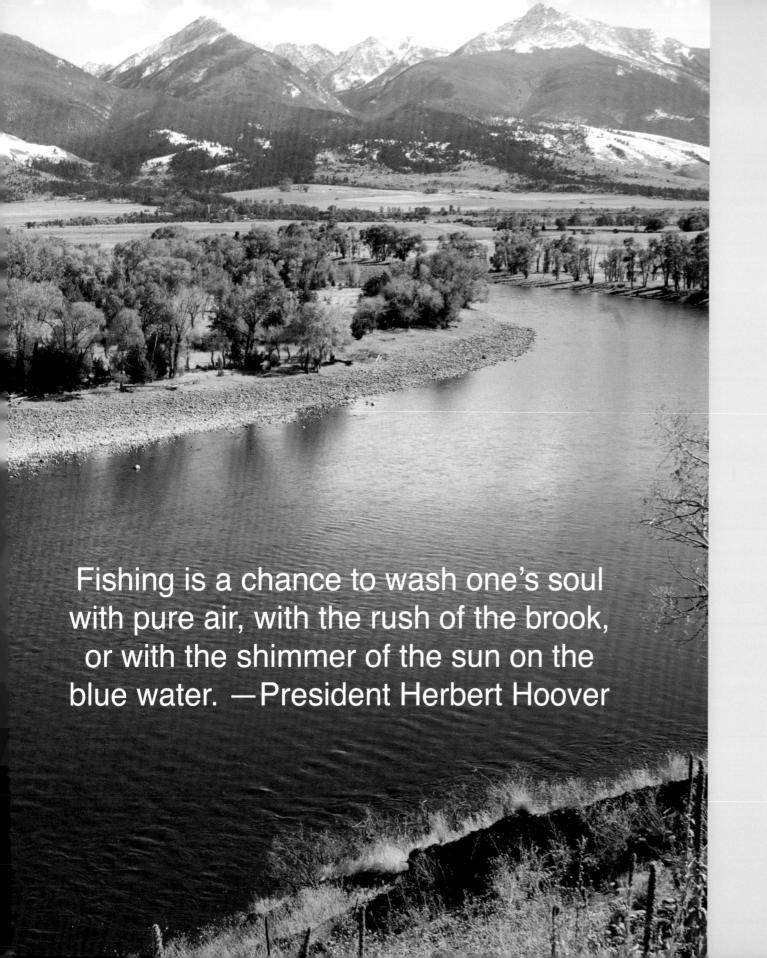

Fishing is a chance to wash one's soul with pure air, with the rush of the brook, or with the shimmer of the sun on the blue water. —President Herbert Hoover

In the land of caribou and ptarmigan lives some
of the world's greatest brook trout fishing.
Welcome to Quebec's fishing treasures.

Vive La Brook Trout
A Journey To Quebec's Leaf River
In Search Of The End Of The Rainbow

t appears the boulders several hundred feet below the floats of our Otter are moving, as if I didn't dose with enough Dramamine and am succumbing to the delirium of motion sickness. Instead, it is a sprawling herd of caribou that stretches to the horizon. More and more animals become visible as if a landscape-sized Polaroid is developing before my eyes. In the distance, the Leaf River snakes across the scruff of northern Quebec, a landscape of barren granite and the occasional copse of black spruce. From the air, it resembles the blotchy salt and pepper complexion of a middle-aged man in need of a shave.

It's been a half-hour since we've seen any hint of man—no trapper cabins, no cut lines to bring power to remote villages, no boats on the lakes below. In contemporary North America—or almost anywhere on the planet for that matter—going past the end of the road has become increasingly difficult. Thus, I savor the view for if landscapes can be endangered, certainly untrammeled wilderness is high atop the list.

The waters of the Leaf are a liquid time capsule of sorts. The river has remained unaffected by man since the last glaciers surrendered their grip on the territory, about the time when wooly mammoth and saber-tooth still roamed

Endless waters of the Leaf River provide mixed blessings of brook trout, lakers and Atlantic salmon, all within easy reach of the Leaf River Outfitters camp.

this land. I have come here in search of an angler's motherlode, with as much hope in my heart as any Forty-Niner or intrepid Klondike explorer. The riches for which I am prospecting, however, are the brook trout that crowd the Leaf, providing fly anglers with the chance to cast in their dreams.

Our destination is Alain Tardiff's tent village on the banks of the Leaf. It is the northernmost outpost in Quebec and an angler's Shangri-La if ever there was one. It's August and the fish are in full spawning attire, dazzling anglers with a riot of red, yellow, violet and coffee with cream. They are pieces of the rainbow captured in piscatorial magnificence, a fish the way Elton John would dress it. They are to trout (even though they're a char) what the wood duck is to waterfowl or the pheasant to upland birds.

For the average Yank who first caught a brook trout on garden hackle in a New England stream narrow enough to stride from bank to bank, places like Quebec and Labrador represent the greatest brook trout fishing on Earth. The cigar-sized fish many of us first hooked south of the Canadian line give way to five- and six-pound fish in the north country.

The world record—a 14-pound lake-run behemoth caught in 1915 on Ontario's Nipigon River—is so outsized from the fish that most of us know as brook trout that it scarcely seems the same species. The mention of Labrador's Minipi or Quebec's Mistassini will bring a Cheshire grin to any fly fisher with a fancy for jaw-dropping brookies.

The fish thrive in frigid waters—from high mountain lakes in the Rockies to the icy waters of Patagonia. They spawn from late August in the far North to December in their southern U.S. range (Georgia and Alabama). Even at the end of summer, the waters of the Leaf are numbingly cold, freezing my hand and turning it to something of an eagle's talon as I reach in to release the first fish of the foray.

All the colors of the rainbow in one glorious fish. While you may have grown up on a diet of cigar-sized brookies in a small New England or Midwestern stream, these members of the char genus routinely reach three to five pounds in the Leaf.

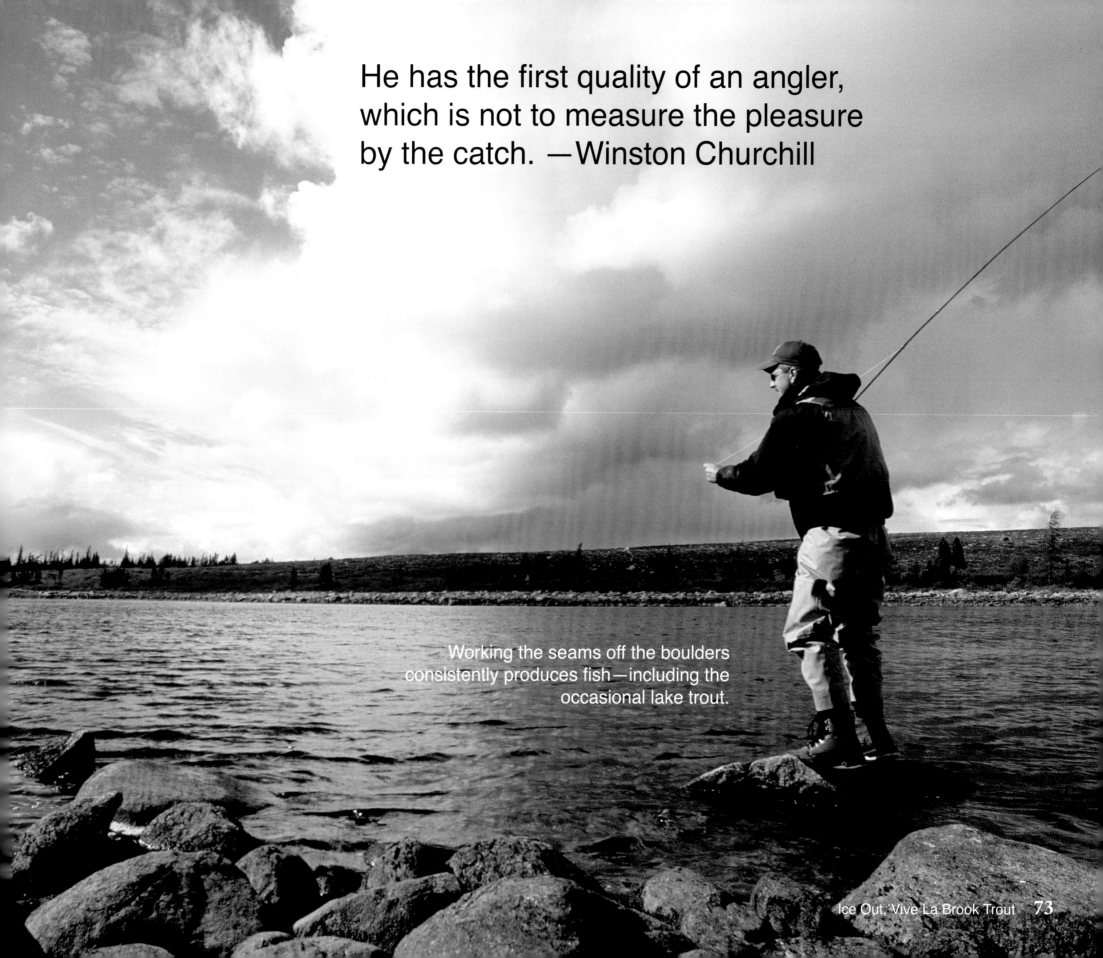

He has the first quality of an angler, which is not to measure the pleasure by the catch. —Winston Churchill

Working the seams off the boulders consistently produces fish—including the occasional lake trout.

Heated tents with wooden floors and comfortable beds delivered unexpected luxury so far from civilization. Warm bathrooms complete with hot showers and a dining lounge made for a welcoming setting after a day on the water—especially after snowy and wet conditions.

I am casting dry flies and catching fish at a rate of 15 an hour—a most leisurely pace at that. It seems as if I might catch just as many on a cotton ball as a fly, for these fish are simpletons that seem hell-bent on feasting before the long, cold winter that will soon descend on this landscape. There's something endearing about going to a place where the fish and game hasn't been jaded by others of the hook-and-bullet fraternity, whether it be waterfowl at the top of the flyway or virgin brook trout.

Behind me, guide Alex Anderson surveys the hills for caribou, for soon he will be taking American sports to the surrounding highlands to stalk the region's abundance of bulls. In the distance, a band of 30 caribou marches single file to the banks of the river. Without pausing, they plow into the water, swimming to new lichen pastures on the other side and, at the same time, answering the ice-age old question of why the caribou crossed the river? Their sweeping racks look like a line of rocking chairs fording the river until they emerge on the far side, shake off and continue to graze up the bank.

There comes a point in my umpteenth cast that catching these magnificent fish just seems too easy, that somehow the experience is cheapened because of the embarrassment of riches. Then I remember the many hours that I spent prospecting mosquito-infested streams in my native Wisconsin for the outside chance of seeing a number 22 dry disappear in a splash no bigger than that made by a dragon fly. I am a helluva long way from home and came here to experience exactly what the Leaf is delivering, penance be damned.

An early episode of *Sports Afield on Assignment* featured the combination of Quebec caribou hunting and brook trout fishing.

The excess of the moment is accentuated when Anderson grabs a 14-inch brookie at the end of my line and matter-of-factly knocks it on the head, the fish's mass quivering for a moment before going limp. The brookie will soon join two of its brethren, released in a pool of smoking oil as Anderson prepares that most celebrated of Canadian events, the shore lunch.

The act of killing a brook trout—or several—feels as if it must have sent a shudder through the fly-fishing force. Elsewhere, the little fish are cupped gently in an angler's hands for a moment to be admired like a work of art before being softly released back to the waters that surrendered it. For Anderson, it's the protein on a plate otherwise laden with carbs.

Lake trout, another member of the genus *Salvelinus*, provide the mix in the cocktail that is Quebec fishing.

The notion of eating a brook trout might seem sacrilegious to some, but when the river is full of them and you're tired of dining on caribou in its many forms, the fish provide a nice addition of surf in a diet otherwise dominated by turf.

have yet to taste a member of the char family that I didn't like—including an ancient 30- to 40-year-old Northwest Territory lake trout that I devoured years ago after six days of eating nothing but caribou in its various forms: tongue, heart, liver and rump roast. No gourmand has ever anticipated any meal more than I did that laker.

Anderson finishes preparing the fish, beans and fried potatoes. He scoops all three onto a plate and hands it to me with a fork and salt shaker as though he's the short order cook at the corner diner. I take in the deliciousness of the lunch and the view, adding a cold beer to complete the perfection of the moment. At the bottom of the plastic container housing our utensils is a sack with two sandwiches consisting of white bread, baloney and some mayo that acts as a binding agent. After a season of brook trout shore lunches, the fish become Anderson's caribou of sorts, proving that diversity is the spice of life, a basic urge even Adam probably felt in the Garden.

Anderson finishes packing plates and pans and shoves us off before piloting the boat to a calm pool within stone-skipping distance of a rapids. It is an ideal lie for brookies looking to fatten themselves before the onset of winter. It also is a place where Anderson has guided scores of other anglers with wanderlust to its vein of piscatorial gold.

step knee deep into the pool and cast. Almost instantly, I feel the tug of a fish, only this time the beast heads for the deep recesses of the main channel. The torque doubles my 6-weight as if I'm woefully under armed for the encounter, clearly I am not wrestling a brook trout this time. Ten minutes later, after mustering as much pressure as seemed prudent, the large form of a 10-pound laker emerges, tired from the struggle and ready to tap out.

I fish my way to waist-deep water, catching three cock brook trout and one hen. Before leaving for another pool, however, I manage one more cast and hook a salmon grilse that leaps spectacularly into the air just as it one day will when it returns from the sea as an adult. The remote waters of the Leaf host strong Atlantic salmon runs each spring and fall and the devotees of the fish have secretly coveted the river for decades. For a growing number of brook trout fishermen who have plied these waters, mums the word as well.

Having the excuse of fishing to take you to untrammeled corners of the globe is perhaps the sport's greatest gift. As I wade the waters of the Leaf, I feel forever indebted to these brook trout that brought me to my own private piece of the tundra . . . a place I will take with me and covet when I return to the world made by men and machines.

What to Bring

Rods and Reels: 3-weight

Lines: Weight-forward

Flies: Start with attractors like Royal Wulff and Coachman, then move to streamers

Other Essential Gear: Fishing rigs for salmon and lake trout

Don't Forget to Pack: Waders

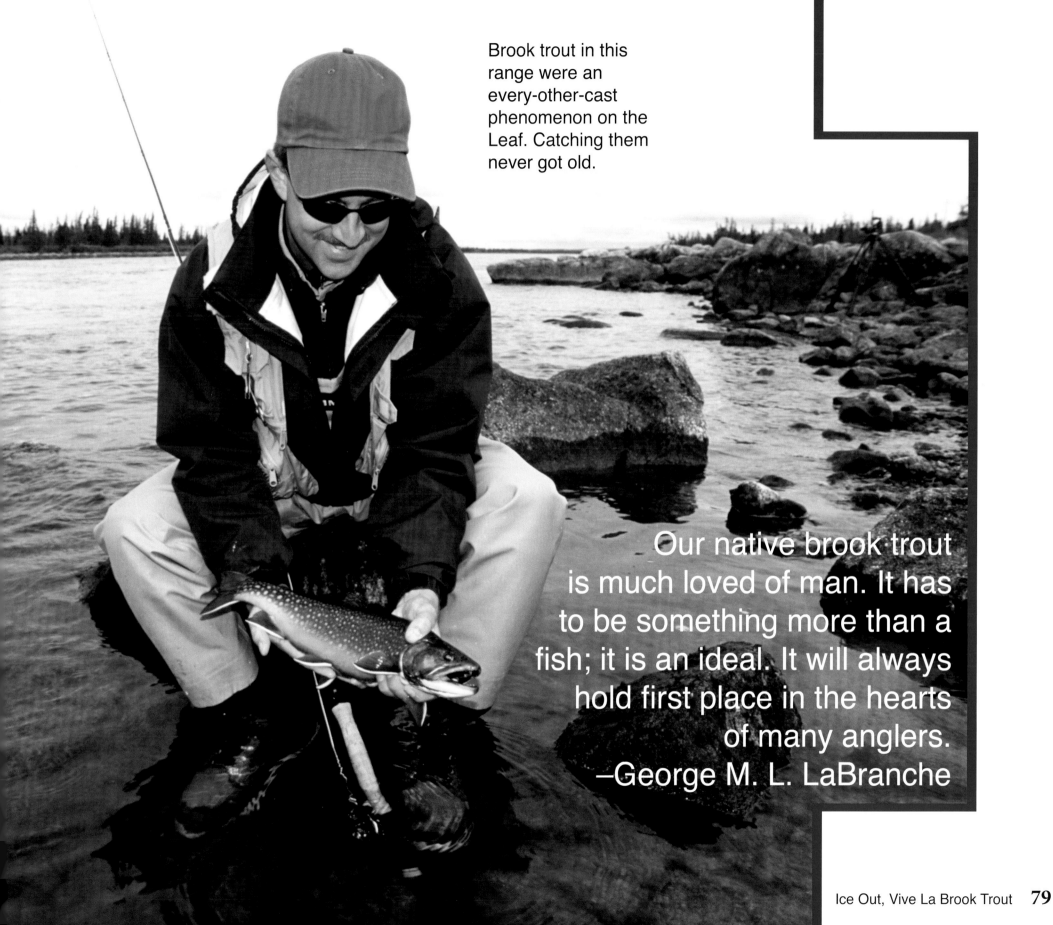

Brook trout in this range were an every-other-cast phenomenon on the Leaf. Catching them never got old.

Our native brook trout is much loved of man. It has to be something more than a fish; it is an ideal. It will always hold first place in the hearts of many anglers.
–George M. L. LaBranche

The Leaf River of northern Quebec is a wilderness paradise for both hunters and anglers.

Float planes are the only way into this stretch of Quebec that is long past the end of the road.

To those devoid of imagination a blank
place on the map is a useless waste;
to others, the most valuable part.
—Charles Dickens

Fly-out fishing forays from Thunderbird
can deliver you to some of the continent's
best pike and walleye fishing.

Northern Exposure
A Return To The Jurassic
For Manitoba's Savage Pike

Taxonomists catalog fishermen in two distinct orders: meat anglers and thrill seekers. If you fall in the ranks of adrenaline junkie, few fish rate higher on the scale than pike, a freshwater barracuda if ever there was one. They are a toothy Jurassic leftover—a malevolent beast likely unthawed from a long forgotten gene pool. The savage predators terrorize their quicksilver neighborhoods like street thugs. Hook one and you're hard wired to a world once ruled by T-Rex.

The sight of a pike heading shark-like to my surface fly raises my hackles like seeing a car about to collide with another. I hold my breath and brace for impact. Pike lie in wait. At the opportune moment, they cock their bodies like a leopard crouching before it pounces on an impala, the fish launching to their prey at speeds approaching 30-miles per hour. Witnessing and feeling such predatory awesomeness is the reason I'm headed north to cast about some of Manitoba's best pike and walleye waters. Leading my tour is Chris Clements, a dealer of sorts who fishes for anglers to convert to addicts of his remote lodges.

Thunderbird Lodge sits on Wrong Lake, a 15-by-six-mile body of pike and walleye heaven that would make any Dardevle chucker or jig fisherman drool. Nothing against spin fishermen (I am one), but I've packed an 11-weight fly rod to subdue the 20-pound brutes that are often found here as well as an 8-weight rod in case we happen upon any eight- to 10-pound walleyes that roam these same waters. The largest pike ever taken on a fly rod—a 33-pound, six-ounce monster—was caught on Manitoba's Lake Nejanilini in 1994, so the region's reputation for producing leviathans is well documented.

Author Chuck Petrie uses a sinking line to retrieve a shore lunch of walleye as guide Chris Clements looks on.

Joining me on the fly-rod adventure is old friend and writer Chuck Petrie, a veteran of the pike-on-the-fly wars who has hooked many of the beasts and lived to tell about it. Clements steers our Lund into a cove collared by dead rushes. We are here just two weeks after ice-out, and we can practically hear the faint stomach growls of the lake's hungry pike as Clements cuts the motor and we drift into the shallow pike zone where the fish are unthawing from a winter spent under the ice, like bottles of vodka stored in a freezer.

I unlimber my 11-weight and tie a starling-sized red and white streamer to the end of my wire leader, figuring a 120 million cream and crimson Dardevles manufactured over the last generation can't be wrong. I false cast until I reach the 60 feet necessary to pitch the fly on the edge of the rushes where I hope to set the table for a famished pike. Within seconds of my third cast hitting the water, a six-pound fish porpoises onto my fly as if style points matter when consuming prey. Once hooked, the pike turns the calm bay into a scene most common on the saltwater flats—where a black-tip might be ravaging a bonefish. Even as small as this pike is, it sends a charge down my rod and up my arm, leaving me to ponder if I'm ready for a 20-pounder. Unlike finicky muskies, pike are voracious and opportunistic feeders and readily attack flies and almost anything else small enough to be swallowed.

About the time I survey the damage to my fly, Petrie sets a hook into what is undoubtedly a 15-pound-plus pike that rips out of the rushes leaving a boat-sized wake in its path. The engagement lasts a few seconds before the fish breaks it off. The waters of Wrong Lake are the color of tea, so sight casting to pike in the shallows is mostly impossible, unlike the opportunities some other clear water destinations offer. The lake, however, is opaque enough to watch a pike strike a submerged fly, an underwater ambush that rivals any apex saltwater game fish.

The deep, cold glacier-carved lakes lined by granite bluffs provide classic habitat for an abundance of pike, walleye and lake trout.

A view of ideal walleye habitat.
Fillet, coat in panko, fry and serve.
Don't forget a beer.

I catch several more hammer-handle-sized pike on successive casts before dropping my fly in the midst of a stand of dead rushes. Caterpillar-sized baitfish shoot out of the water behind my fly as though popcorn is bursting from the surface, the effects of the reverse polarity caused by an approaching northern. The piscatorial torpedo heads for my imitation, smacking with the intensity not heretofore felt on 30 previous pike hookups. In an instant, the fish has taken me into the backing as I fight it off the reel, cupping my left hand to create a makeshift drag as the fish heads to a murky pool beneath a house-sized granite boulder. Ten minutes later, Clements releases the 17-pound fish back to the waters of Wrong Lake. It's still not the 20-pound pike we hope to catch, but it is nevertheless a lot of fish on a fly.

A first glance at the lake and one would assume that it would hold muskies as well as pike, but while the fish share many similarities, the pike favor much colder water. Muskies prefer water in the 67- to 72-degree range while pike—especially large pike—do best in water ranging from 50 to 55 degrees. They're truly fish of the north. The largest specimens come from the cold glacial lakes of northern Canada and Europe, where the bulk of the planet's supply of vodka originates . . . coincidence? Muskies, on the other hand, are only found in lower latitudes of North America—mostly beer country.

We return to the lodge for lunch and the opportunity to quiz the other anglers in camp—conventional tackle devotees—about their luck with pike. We discover that two fish over 45 inches were caught and another 50-inch fish made it as far as the edge of the boat only to flop off the hook before a net could be retrieved. That's their stories, anyway, and they're sticking to them.

No matter how good the fishing is, it's never better than shore lunch. Everything stops when walleye is served.

After gorging ourselves on deep fried walleye--like pike at an all-you-can-eat minnow buffet—we return to the lake, only this time we unleash our 8-weight rods and sinking tips as we prospect for shallow water walleyes. While a fly angler won't match the production of a jig fisherman (and it's much easier to drink beer while dunking a jig) a five- or six-pound walleye on a fly rod is nevertheless a memorable event. Spring and fall are generally the only periods when walleyes are shallow enough to be reached with fly line, provided you can get a fly past the ever-present pike that are prone to intercepting it before it reaches walleye depth.

Legions of fly fishers have become hooked on sight casting to aggressive pike. Here Clements releases a 15-pounder.

Petrie is the first to hook a walleye of any note, a 20-inch fish stained a golden copper from the lake's tannin waters. Clements, using jigs, soon lands a 24-inch fish that makes some of our earlier walleyes look like bait by comparison. Even the lake's largest walleyes, however, are scarred from pike teeth as walleyes provide a substantial portion of the diet of the lake's resident pike population.

At one point, Petrie tussles with what appears to be a large walleye only to discover that the fish was perhaps but a three-pounder. Fresh tooth marks on the side of the walleye told the story of the pike mugging the walleye experienced on the way to the boat. The effect was 15 pounds worth of fight for several moments.

The greediness of pike knows no bounds.
—Sergei Aksakov

Nothing in the world of freshwater fishing strikes a fly any harder than a pike— including muskies.

Mornings until about 11a.m. are spent casting for pike. Then it's time to catch lunch— and that means walleye.

Nobody with a full stringer of fish goes home by the way of the back alley.
–Mark Twain

Leech, mayfly and minnow imitations are good medicine for walleyes, and anyone who has ever tasted the species fresh from the water knows why the shore lunch was invented in the first place. After landing several two-pound fish before noon, we head to a rocky point where a stone fire pit is waiting along with large skillets that will be the offshore habitat of the tender walleye fillets that Clements dredges in a mixture of seasonings, cornmeal and flour. If there is a fish that tastes better than fresh walleye at a shore lunch, please submit your nominations.

After lunch, we return to another shallow bay in search of pike. Fighting a strong wind, we manage to catch several northerns in the 10-pound class on surface flies that we snake through the rushes with fast strips, creating splashes that approximate a struggling mouse. The 20-pounders, though, elude us. Somewhere in the murky depths those leviathans are watching and waiting for just the right ambush.

It's the legend of these giant pike that'll continue to haunt me until I once again return to the north country and its Jurassic waters. It's just a spring thaw away. 🌀

What to Bring

Rods and Reels: Six-foot six-inch or taller medium-heavy casting rod and reel

Lines: 12- to 20-pound-test with 24-inch wire leaders

Flies and Lures: Barbless hooks are required in Manitoba

Other Essential Gear: Fishing rigs for walleye and perch

Don't Forget to Pack: Extra layers

Can't catch walleye on a fly? Think again. Just add sinking line and default to a red and white pattern.

Petrie angles for a hefty pike holding near shore.

It wouldn't be a Canadian fly-in fishing trip without workhorse of the northcountry, the de Havilland Beaver.

Many men go fishing all their lives without knowing that it is not fish they are after.
—Henry David Thoreau

That is winter steelheading:
long hours of cold, interminable
work, punctuated with breath-
less moments of excitement.
—Steve Raymond'

Steel Resolve

The Pere Marquette Serves Up What Lake Michigan Delivers

'm in the bow of a johnboat working my way upstream, feeling like a governor surveying a disaster area. More than 300 inches of snow has landed on this part of Michigan in a record dump that looks as if Mount Vesuvius has just buried Pompeii in ash. As we boat around each bend, what looks like snow-covered hills are actually just piles of snow troweled by restless winds. It's clear spring is going to be late this year-—like July late. Not that the river's steelhead could care.

The stream amounts to a fish trail cut into the snow. It's the kind of woodland waterway that I grew up along in southern Wisconsin, only the intensive agriculture around us with its moldboard plowing, heavy fertilizers and kill-every-hopper pesticides stunted the river. Only creek chubs, carp, and occasional suckers (*aka anglers*) called its silted—and jilted—waters home.

As we serpentine our way down the river, the naked tentacles of hardwood stems appear ghostly as they stretch like ghoulish hands from the snow. In the faint gray light, the barren forest looks as if it has been burned, the skeletal remains of maple and dogwood whose trunks lie dormant, awaiting spring and a fresh infusion of sap to resuscitate them back to life.

With spring and fall runs of hard-fighting steelhead and salmon, the PM, as locals call it, is a gem among American fisheries.

If this float were merely described to me, I'd feel like I am drifting Hemingway's Big Two-Hearted, that storied stream of consciousness that descends from the literary watershed originating in Walden Pond. This river, however, is named for French Father Jacques Marquette, the Jesuit Priest who explored these waters some 300 years ago. The Pere Marquette flows 64 miles with its tributaries of the Little South and Middle Branch meeting to create the main river that eventually spills into Lake Michigan.

It's a relatively modest Midwest stream that looks like the kind of creeks I used to fish for cigar-sized native brook trout or the occasional brown trout. The notion that 10-pound steelhead (a few get double that size) and 20- to 30-pound chinook make annual runs up these waters—to say nothing of the wild browns that are here year round—makes the fishing in the Pere Marquette seem as unbelievable as a fish tale. I am here in need of evidence.

For Dan Flavin, a Michigan native who has seemingly been in the automobile advertising business since he was driving Hot Wheels, a journey to the PM, as locals call it, is at least an annual affair. He had been coaxing me to join him for a long time on these waters, enticing me with photo after photo of outsized steelhead and salmon—always feeling like photo-shopped images of what looked like Pacific Northwest fish in a Great Lakes woodland setting. Given the background, each time I examined one of the photos I could almost hear the drumming of a grouse or the jackhammering of a pileated woodpecker. If the photo could produce an aroma it would have undoubtedly been a mix of decaying leaves and rotting wood, the smell that signals the morels to pop in time for turkey hunters to harvest them.

Soon we float to a pool formed by a bend in the river where we could see perhaps 100 fish lying motionless at the bottom like so many forgotten boat anchors. I begin casting slightly upriver and let my fly drift the periphery of the school. On my third cast, one brute of a fish separates from the school to take the fly.

Suddenly, what I presume would be a sluggish fish owing to the coldness of the water transforms into a beast auditioning for role of tarpon. It takes me far downriver as guide Mike Whittle begins hurdling through the water on an intercept course with net in hand to the hooked torpedo. Whittle has been guiding for years in these parts, sharing this spirited river's riches of steelhead, chinook salmon and brown trout to anyone willing to listen to his testimonials about the quality of its fishing.

Veteran fly fisher Dan Flavin hoists one of nearly a dozen steelhead he landed in one day on the Pere Marquette.

Any person who does not fish is bordering on the psychotic. He is a poor, abnormal creature from another world who may know how to make a living but who does not know how to live. —Philip Rice

Experience usually is what you get when you don't get what you want, but if there were no such thing as optimism there wouldn't be any such thing as fishing. —Michael McIntosh

Tie into a steelhead and you will experience the body builders of the trout world, their sheer strength and yearning for freedom born of a more savage big water ecosystem, just like their coastal cousins whose survival skills are honed in the Pacific and Atlantic dodging everything from seals to orcas. Combine their innate strength and substantial heft with their habit of turning downriver to harness the current and it makes fighting a steelhead the fishing equivalent of calf roping. When it comes to acrobatic prowess, the fish seem to take a page out of the Atlantic salmon playbook, putting on aerial displays that add spectacle and theater—to say nothing of adrenaline—to the experience. This is the narcotic of steelhead fishing and why the species has such a following of anglers always in need of a fix.

Feeding on a steady diet of alewives or rainbow smelt, Great Lakes steelhead mature in two to three years and most return to their natal waters (whether hatched or released) between late October and early May, with the peak of spawning for the fish that enter the river in the fall occurring in mid-April.

Spring on the PM comes in a mix of weather systems. But the fish pay no attention—nor do savvy anglers.

Fishing is a world created apart
from all others, and inside it are
special worlds of their own. . .
. —Norman Maclean

When you see the PM for the first time, it's hard to fathom the depth of the fishery and the size of the beasts that lurk in these relatively small waters.

The vein of silvery fish beneath us delivers all day, as the sun hits the river and it warms a bit, they become ever-more active. Later in the morning, I watched a chinook-sized fish slip between the other steelhead, moving in almost slow motion as it parked on the edge of the school. It was an invitation I couldn't resist, so I dropped my fly six feet ahead of the brute and let the current do the rest of the work. It rose to my Clown Egg as I watched it open its mouth and inhale the offering, the hook coming to rest firmly in the crook of its maw.

This fish was to the rest of the school what a brown bear is to a grizzly. The freakish creature plowed downriver, jumping in crescents out of the water as if it was stitching the river with my line. Ten minutes later and 100 yards downstream, the leviathan finally comes to net in what was the epic engagement of my PM exploration.

When the steelhead first enter the PM from Lake Michigan, their backs are green and their bottoms silver. As they prepare to spawn, however, their rainbow colors become more prominent until the red splash on their sides and prominent polka dots signal that they are ready for their nuptial dance to begin.

While steelhead were first introduced to the Great Lakes in the 1870s from California's McCloud River to the famed Au Sable, the current fishery is the result of concerted stocking programs that began in the 1960s. Today, the PM and other Michigan streams are the deliverers of angling dreams, truly astounding fisheries that Father Marquette could have only dreamed of experiencing. And once you hook a steelhead here, you'll never cross a bridge in these parts without wondering what angling might await below. 🐟

What to Bring

Rods & Reels: Nine-foot medium-fast or fast action for 10-weight

Lines: Floating lines, 10- to 12-pound test tippet

Flies: Nymphs and eggs

Other Essential Gear: extra-large landing net

Don't Forget to Pack: Tape measure

Guide Mike Whittle joins me to memorialize one of the brutes that took me to the backing and nearly 100 yards downstream.

2 ▷▷▷

THE WEST

In the land of drifters, ne'er-do-wells and other fishermen

Fly fishing is to fishing as ballet is to walking. —Howell Raines

Flip Pallot invites a Big Hole River brown to the party.

Grip your oars, men and clutch your souls! –Herman Melville

Huey Lewis has found his new drug on Montana's Big Hole. The river, like many in Montana, has seen its struggles over water rights.

Requiem For A River
Saying Goodbye To The Currents Of Time

I didn't think it was possible to fall in love with a river, but that's what happened the first time I met Montana's Big Hole. Everything about this river seemed perfect to me. It moved with a captivating grace and brought endless smiles, joy and peace.

After a long absence, my heart was always full to see it again, like an embrace with an old friend. When the headwinds of life seemed especially stiff, its current brought solace, forever a steady force reminding me to separate fleeting from enduring. My friends all loved the river, too, meeting it brought them the same happiness I first experienced more than a decade ago. Like a generous soul, it gave of itself and never asked for anything in return. Now, however, it is time to say goodbye, even though a part of me doesn't want to let go. I wonder if life will bring me to these waters again, and I ponder whether there's truth in Frost's assertion that *nothing gold can stay.*

The relationship started on one of those crisp Montana autumn days, cobalt blue skies with the cottonwoods dressed in lemon sequins, shimmering in the sunlight letting you know that she was ready to dance. If you've ever driven past the Big Hole River in late September and early October, you know just how irresistible it can be. Seductive, really. Trout have to win a lottery to call this river home, so when you ease to its bank to make your first cast, you do so with some trepidation of rejection. *Am I worthy of these fish,* I wonder?

I waded to a riffle that ran in the late afternoon shadow of a cut bank, willows partly shielding it from sight of the area's ospreys. I dropped a hopper at the top of the short run, not needing to mend my line for 20 feet or maybe a bit more. Perhaps two seconds into the drift, the fly disappeared with hardly a disturbance on the surface, as if it simply passed into a parallel universe through some undetectable worm hole.

George Goody tries his luck on a back channel of the Big Hole as Pallot looks on—along with a million viewers of a series called *Fishing Frontiers* that we produced with the legendary host.

clenched the line in what amounted to a simple reflex at the fly's vanishing. Then my rod bent hard and fast as a still unseen fish was protesting its way down river, seemingly looking to make off with the purse it just snatched. In that moment, I pictured the scene as a passing eagle might, as Shilstone might have painted it. It was an out-of-body moment that I had never experienced fishing before or since.

The Big Hole River had whispered in my ear . . . that it was time to come home to her waters.

That began a series of restless days and nights—months and years, really. That's the way many of us come to Montana, for the journey often starts in the spirit before we're moved to find a place to call home. With enough money saved and my wife convinced that it would be okay to share me with the river, we set out to find our piece of Montana along the banks of the Big Hole where I could draw strength from her life force each day I was there.

What started as a simple cabin became something more, probably too much. When you come to the banks of a river, however, you aren't

buying property as much as you are a dream. It is an acknowledgement of the power of a river and the cosmic draw of its currents. It became a place for our families and many friends to come and meet the Big Hole, to appreciate how this timeless water nurtures us.

One of those souls was my older sister who would sit each morning by the big window that faced the river, staring out looking for deer, the occasional moose that would wander through or a bald eagle that liked this view for the same reasons we did. She also seemed to be looking for answers, for she was dying of breast cancer and the river provided a kind of treatment that she couldn't find in an urban hospital. Her soul seemed to strengthen even as her body weakened. Nothing heals like creation therapy and as any fly fisher will tell you, more than line is mended on a river. I do not know what she saw when she died, but I hope it was a vision of the Big Hole in its autumn glory, a place where heaven can't be more than a roll cast away.

My sons became anglers and riverkeepers on this water, mostly thanks to friends and guides named George, Eric, Ryan, Rick and several others who cared enough to teach along the way. They saw in my twins the same wonder and awe they knew at that age, the intrigue and curiosity in how it all worked from the fly to the fish to the hope of more to come.

We shared the Big Hole with so many friends as well, in many cases people who came from faraway lands and cities, people who had heard of Montana but didn't know that it was a state of mind until they arrived. Baptizing souls to this river became one of the great joys of my life, for people who spent a day on the river returned to our home renewed, understanding the draw of these currents and just how endearing they could be.

Then something changed. The river became stingy, seldom sharing the numbers of fish she once

Son Luke and guide Eric Thorson celebrate a handsome brown early in our tenure on the Big Hole.

did. Drifts that used to produce 30 or more fish—a mix of rainbows, browns, the occasional brook trout and grayling—now delivered less than a dozen. While we used to count on a fish or two over 18 inches each time we floated, few made it past 14 anymore. Some floats never saw more than a ruler's length trout, if any at all. Before we knew it, we were counting whitefish in our daily totals.

That's when I began to notice what was happening. *How could I have been so oblivious to what the Big Hole was enduring,* I began to think to myself. Trees were being cut along its shores, the banks and the brush that help protect favorite trout lairs were being burned for no more reason than to meet the vision of someone's river aesthetic, as if the Big Hole wasn't already perfect in its natural form. A little nip-tuck here and there that is seldom noticed until the river is no longer recognizable, until the trout homes were gone or abandoned under a layer of silt.

Fog adds to the mystery that shrouds the Big Hole. What will the future hold for this epic waterway?

Then came the lust for a third crop of hay. Fly the Big Hole Valley in the hot, often dry days of August and an Incan-like series of sprinklers and irrigation canals bleed the Big Hole daily, siphoning water levels so low that there is no longer enough oxygen to support trout. The state's answer for this is to stop angling to reduce stress on the fish, as if the way to cure the disease is to treat the symptom, not the cause.

As any honest rancher will tell you, the third crop of hay is the weakest, sometimes not worth the time and energy—to say nothing of water—to grow it. If the river could speak, however, it would ask what of the anglers who come to Montana to meet its fish? Fishermen spend nearly $1 billion annually here, fueling the entire rural economy that includes restaurants, gas stations, fly shops, grocery stores, bars, guides and outfitters, lodges and scores of other enterprises. To suggest that this is only a debate between ranching and fishing, which is a common refrain, is to say that the fight is only about the golden egg, not the goose that laid it and all who profit from it.

Furthermore, cattle and hay ranching employs few people in Montana; most operations are run by a small number of individuals who now ride machines instead of horses. Cattle processing, for the most part, is done out of state, in Nebraska and Iowa, so Montana doesn't even benefit from the jobs created by its own beef production.

I do not believe any of this is an orchestrated, sinister plot to rob the Big Hole and other Montana rivers of their treasures, however. I do not think ranchers are evil people intent on killing every fish in the river so that they never have to hear the complaints of anglers and guides. Rather, there is simply more demand than ever to extract dollars out of each acre of ground and anyone and anything—anglers and trout—that get in the way of that mission become an accidental opponent . . . needlessly.

I fell in love with Montana at first sight . . .
And not for the valleys, exactly, but for the
rivers that run through the valleys.
—Charles Kuralt

In late summer, the Big Hole's flow is
often diminished as the head gates
are opened and the valley's wide-
spread sprinkler irrigation is used to
try and produce a third crop of hay.
If water temperatures rise, the state
will close angling to reduce stress
on the fish. Such a move is costly
to many Montana businesses that
depend on fishing tourism.

Yet another fire burns the banks of the Big Hole, destroying riparian habitat vital for trout. The cover also is needed to shade the water in order to keep it cool, key to holding enough oxygen to sustain the river's trout.

While there have been county watershed boards and other groups formed to bring a dialogue between disparate factions, most of these organizations are run by ranchers and ranching interests, and the best outcomes are to try and get ranchers to *voluntarily* decrease their use of river water for the last crop of hay. It's a public face—some would say farce—to ameliorate contention between ranching and fishing interests.

The outcomes, however, are dubious at best, for many ranchers simply disregard such agreements and open their irrigation head gates to the river—often in the cover of darkness—dropping the Big Hole significantly overnight. Thus, the amount of oxygen needed to support trout, and the extended human community around them, declines to the point of killing fish. Rivers don't die overnight and there are no obituaries. Instead, it's a cancerous end as a river chokes and the big fish die one by one, their corpses absorbed by crayfish and other lesser organisms that remove the evidence.

How could this be, you ask? What about federal laws to protect such shared resources? Those are questions more Montanans are asking as well, for the federal Environmental Protection Agency and provisions of the Clean Water Act are in place for just such a backstop. It's the responsibility of Montana's Department of Environmental Quality to enforce those laws. So why aren't they doing their job? Why isn't the legislature demanding that they fulfill their responsibilities?

Tennessee native Mark Ingram hoists a handsome rainbow caught in the Beaverhead near Dillon, Montana.

The view inside our home off the Big Hole, a place where we baptized many souls to the wonders of Montana fishing.

A loss of dissolved oxygen is degrading the Big Hole's water quality and the same problem exists across many of the state's rivers as fishing is often closed in late summer. Those facts are indisputable and painful to the thousands of Montanans whose livelihoods depend on anglers.

Big Hole River guides walk a fine line, for they are selling a product—epic fishing on one of America's last great freestone rivers unspoiled by dams. Who could blame them for not publicly decrying the state of affairs, for to do so is an admission that the fishery, and their offering, is in decline. How can they pay for their rod days without a steady stream of clients? Too, there are always images of plenty of fish that show up in that bastion of truth and clarity known as social media to proclaim the river still the deliverer of fishing dreams. Anyone who has spent consistent time on the Big Hole, however, can separate marketing from reality.

Someday, perhaps, the anglers, guides and the many businesses supported by fishermen will take their rightful place at the head of the table of Montana's river interests. For now, however, the Montana that once was—a state that had become the spiritual center of the fly-fishing universe, brimming with unmatched numbers of trout and angling opportunities—is no longer. Instead, the promise of the Big Hole and other rivers to deliver historic days on the water—the kind that echo through America's fishing community—are mostly just memories, like ghosts of fishermen past.

I will forever cherish my time on the Big Hole, recalling all that it gave to me and my family. Since I first noticed the symptoms, I fought for the river's return to vigor, its very survival. Now, however, I leave that to others who love these waters. As we sell our home on the banks of the Big Hole and say goodbye to a dream, I weep for this river—not for my loss but for those who will never know it as I did, when it was gold.

Perhaps Frost was right, after all.

Sharing the river with guests from across the globe became one of the great joys of our lives. Watching the abuse of the Big Hole worsen, however, has been one of life's great disappointments.

> ### What to Bring
>
> Rods and Reels: 5- or 6-weight
>
> Lines: Sink-tip
>
> Flies: It changes all year long—trust your guide
>
> Other Essential Gear: Waders and boots
>
> Don't Forget to Pack: Watercraft must be inspected when coming in from out of state

For the occasional visitor to the Big Hole, the decline of the river isn't obvious. It's not that there isn't still decent fishing, it's simply not what it once was. Whether it can be returned to its former glory is the question that looms large.

Hope Ingram celebrates a beautiful Beaverhead brown. Though not as attractive as the Big Hole, the Beaverhead's tailwater fishery hasn't suffered as dramatically as the Big Hole in recent years.

Watching my sons learn to love the Big Hole and fight for its protection has brought its own rewards during the struggle to save one of the country's last great freestone waterways.

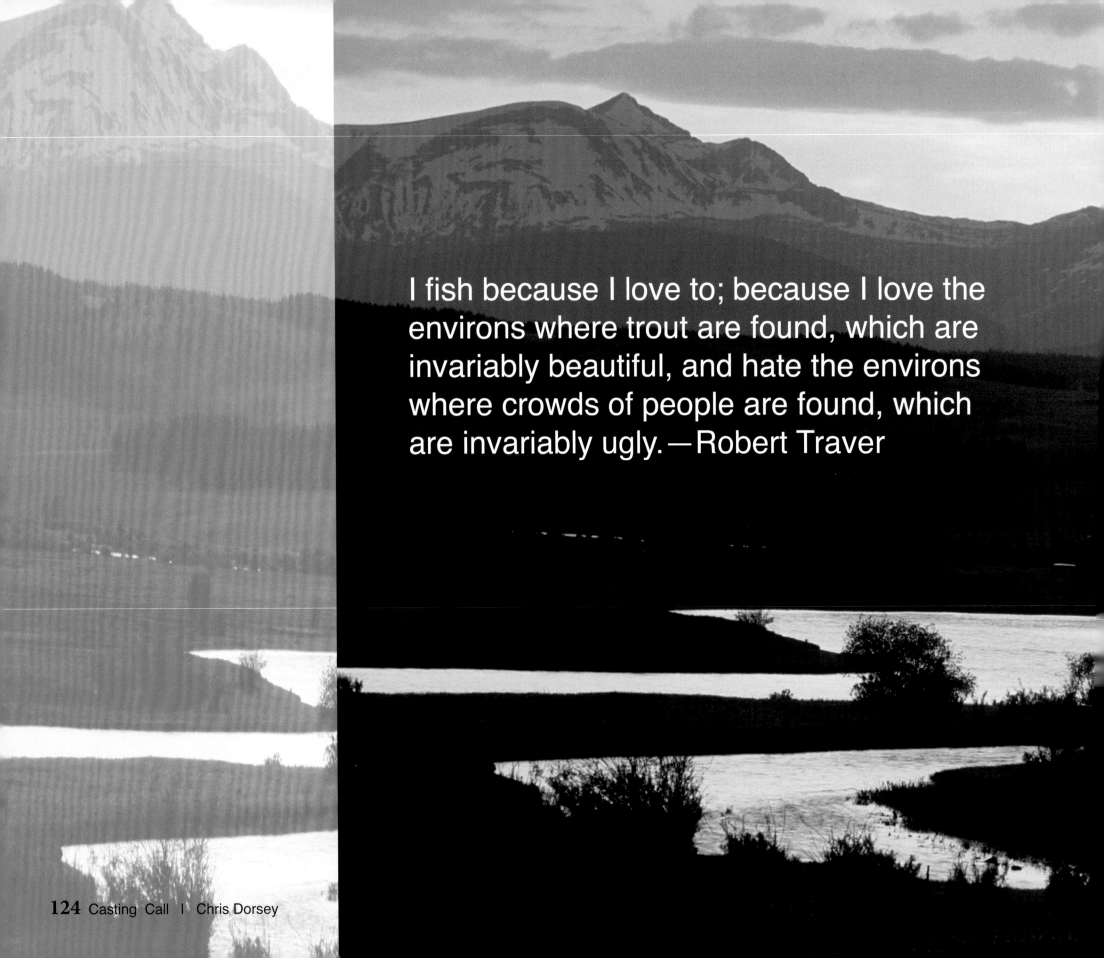

I fish because I love to; because I love the environs where trout are found, which are invariably beautiful, and hate the environs where crowds of people are found, which are invariably ugly. —Robert Traver

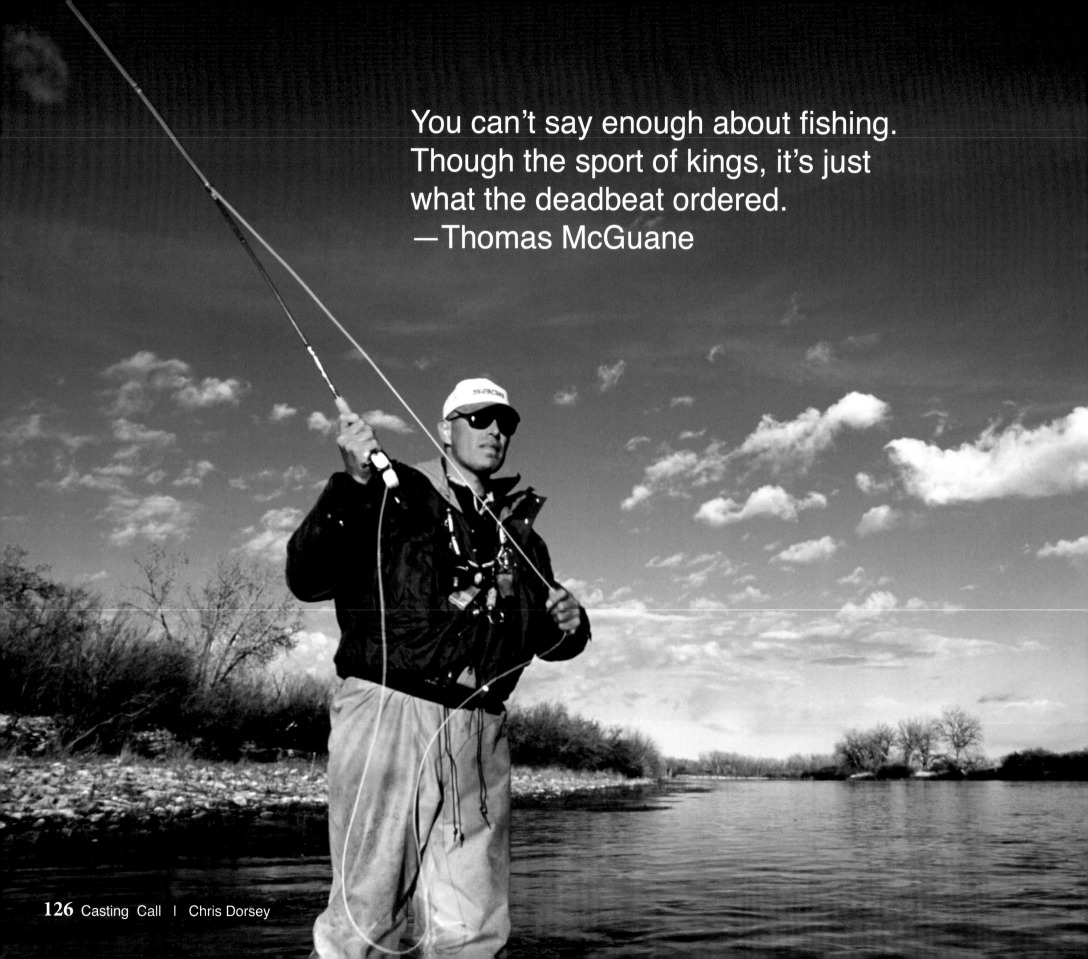

You can't say enough about fishing.
Though the sport of kings, it's just
what the deadbeat ordered.
—Thomas McGuane

Rod & Gun

The Lure Of The Bighorn's Fish And Fowl

Great trout streams are as timeless as a classic book that begs to be read over and over—and that reveals something new with each engagement. To fly fishers, few titles are any more inviting than the Bighorn, a river that sits atop Montana's long list of fly-fishing best sellers. For Bighorn River Lodge's Phil Gonzalez, who grew up along the banks of the Yellowstone River near Billings, there is no better trout stream in North America than the Bighorn. And with some 7,200 trout per river mile, who could argue the point?

While I've fished many of the most celebrated trout waters on the continent, my enduring favorites are the Bighorn and the Missouri—and the Big Hole if the salmonfly hatch delivers. As I find myself seated in a drift boat on the Bighorn with guide Shawn Smith, I prepare for what I'm sure will be another epic day on this tailwater fishery. Some rivers—notably the Big Hole—are schizophrenic, generous one day and stingy the next. The Bighorn, however, seems perpetually rosy . . . just like the mood of its anglers.

Chuck Petrie works to separate a trout from the Bighorn, one of Montana's most productive rivers.

Despite chilly temps, late season trout angling can be remarkably productive in Montana—especially on the Bighorn.

Smith launches the boat below a secondary dam that keeps the Bighorn from swelling out of its banks as many other Montana streams are wont to do during spring run-off. He no sooner rows the drift boat into the deepest stretch of the river than a trout hammers my fly—a no-see-um-sized 22 midge nymph I'm using to mine the cool December waters. The fish tugs violently four times as it torpedoes upriver, jerking my grip as it shakes hands with me via the 5-weight rod. Following the brief introduction, however, it spits the hook and returns to the recesses of the deep pool. We are two minutes into our five-hour float, so the boat is awash in optimism. We are, after all, on the Bighorn.

We pass another angler and guide who've also decided to take advantage of the unseasonably mild temperatures and ideal casting conditions, which is to say no wind. I cast to a calm patch of water amid a 50-yard stretch of riffles. Just as the fly unwinds below the surface, another trout hits my offering, running to the middle of the river before letting me play him to the boat and into Smith's waiting net. It's a gift of 20 inches of rainbow—fat, vigorous and ready to test any angler looking for a fight—the kind of fish for which the Bighorn is world-renowned.

Habitat nearby the Bighorn is resplendent with sharptail grouse and pheasants, making a trip to this piece of Montana in late autumn an ideal cast-and-blast destination.

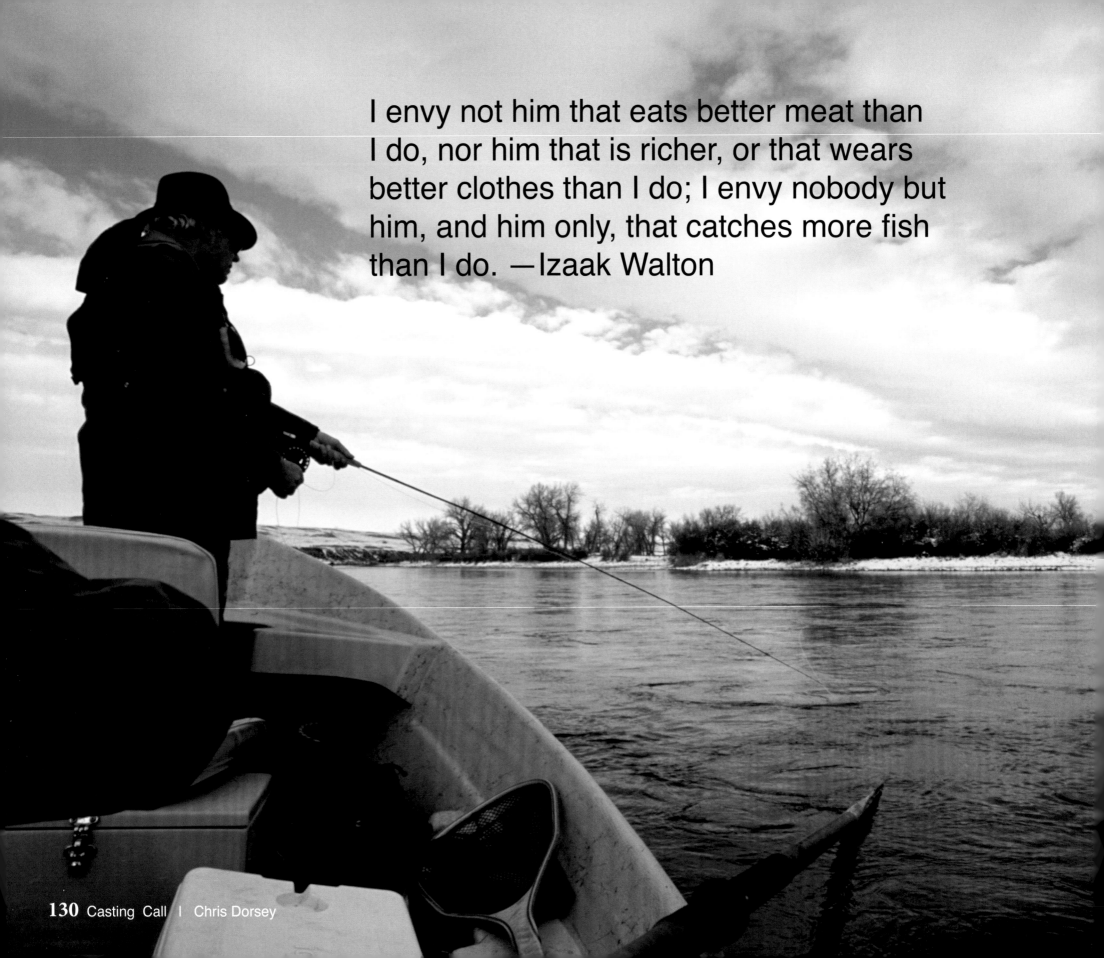

I envy not him that eats better meat than I do, nor him that is richer, or that wears better clothes than I do; I envy nobody but him, and him only, that catches more fish than I do. —Izaak Walton

The tiniest of midges and nymphs are favorite selections for late season floats on the Bighorn.

Bighorn trout are typically in the 16- to 18-inch neighborhood with plenty of outliers. Because of the abundant insect life in and around the river, the fish consume plenty of protein and, consequently, grow at an accelerated rate—as much as three inches a month according to one state of Montana study. While the life expectancy of trout in most Montana streams is about nine years, the hyper growth rate of the Bighorn trout means that few survive longer than six years.

We round another bend, Smith rowing in earnest to position me over a favorite lie before nodding to me to set the table for the trout he's sure are waiting to be served below. I cast, pause, mend my line and watch as my fly vanishes in a blink. I set the hook and finesse a plump brown trout to the surface quickly, but the fish is far from succumbing to my tiny offering and whisker-thin 5X tippet. The fast-action rod is something of a magic wand in my hand. There is electricity in strong fighting fish, and the best rods transfer that energy from the trout to your nerves without any breakers.

I pause to admire the golden hues of the 16-inch brown before returning it to the water so that it can continue with the business of the spawn. Redds are obvious throughout the river bottom, and along the shore I spy a trio of the fish working the gravel as though there is no concern for the ever-present bald and golden eagles that glide overhead. Come spring, it will be time for the rainbows to do the same as the next generation of rod-benders begin their life amid the storied waters of the Bighorn.

Another half dozen trout find their way to my fly before we reach the take-out point, and an equal number play me before slipping off the hook or breaking my tippet. Just as I had hoped, however, the Bighorn gave me a tale to share and one I will remember each time I think of the best of Montana's legendary angling.

As a life-long lover of game birds and gun dogs, I have had a fascination with sharptails from the beginning, for I have come to appreciate the prairie as only a wing shooter and dog trainer could. The Bighorn trip, then, was planned as a cast and blast adventure . . . arguably one of the most epic and dramatic our continent offers. The native grouse I am hunting are descendants of the same birds that saw the first sod-busters roll the dice as they crossed the plains taking their chances on a better life. The birds' leks—the stages upon which they perform their spring court-ship rituals—once rested amid the sea of bison that inhabited these parts.

These same birds inspired the dance of prairie tribes who found magic in their unique courtship display.

Late season angling in Montana means you're likely to have the river to yourself, for the crowds of anglers and rafters have long since departed. Consequently, the fish aren't as shell-shocked and tend to be more receptive to a fly.

Guide Brandon Costley ushers me to a 15,000-deeded-acre ranch operated by newlyweds Dave and Shawna Stevens. It is a vast pasture veined with mile upon mile of wooded ravines that provide a plethora of hiding places for the region's mix of grouse and pheasants.

Costley's young Lab—a 45-pound female named Teton—is ideally suited for the close-in work found in these thickets. I flank one side as Costley negotiates the house-high woody vegetation below. I spy Teton as she spins around a small impenetrable thicket with ears perked and tail moving like a windshield wiper in a downpour. I take my gun out of the crook of my arm and prepare to shoot, for even though the breed isn't known for pointing, her body language is enough to tell me that she's about to come nose to beak with a bird. In an instant, the tops of the thicket begin to tremble as a sharptail makes two attempts to break through the tightly woven canopy before finally succeeding. I spin to the left and take it quartering away in what is a simple shot. Ahead, more birds are flushing, taking the blast as their cue to find new cover . . . and soon.

Teton collects the bird and delivers it matter-of-factly to Costley who grabs it and continues down the draw. We meander another hundred yards when the chatter of grouse can be heard before a flock of the birds launches well ahead of us. All that is left is hot scent and the disbelief in the eyes of young Teton as she can't imagine where all the birds have gone that left the overdose of scent behind. The more I hunt birds, the more I appreciate what a good dog brings to the equation, for they are interpreters telling us the story of birds through their animated reactions to scent.

We decide to move to another draw and let these birds rest. With unmolested grouse and pheasants, we use the same approach to unearth a flock of sharptails within easy range. I take a pair as they reach the pinnacle of the hill ahead of me. Teton disappears as Costley blows his whistle to keep the dog from prospecting too far ahead of us. After a five-minute pause, the dog returns with the second grouse in her jaws.

After lunch, I head up a draw where we had seen a pair of roosters depart to escape our wrath during an earlier drive. Costley works a lower thicket. There is just enough snow on the ground to make tracking possible, so I head to two patches of cover the size of putting greens where I find fresh pheasant tracks, small diamonds in the powder. The tracks meander for 30

Upland birds and waterfowl are found in abundance along the Bighorn, one of the best wing-shooting (and fly-fishing) zones in all of Montana.

A cold day on the water is always made warmer by hot fishing action. With more than 7,000 trout per river mile, few waters deliver more than the Bighorn.

Legendary lodge owner and guide Phil Gonzalez has introduced legions of anglers to the wonders of the Bighorn.

The hope of the evening rise is a
darker, more powerful hope; it is a
mysterious time, when miracles may
happen. —Roderick Haig-Brown

yards before leading to the last of the cover. Unless the birds had already flushed from the area when I wasn't watching, they should be sitting just ahead of me.

I take two more steps and a brace of cock birds and a hen depart in different directions. I swing on the first bird and miss but connect on the second cock. It is a chance for a perfect double, but I settle for the memory of the one that got away instead. It's a recollection that takes me back to the first time I hunted pheasants in a cattail slough more than 30 years ago. While the covers have changed over the years, the narcotic of a flush hasn't.

Combining the continent's best trout fishing with some of the best wing shooting, well, can only mean the Bighorn is nearby. And what a generous river it is.

What to Bring

Rods and Reels: 5-weight for dry flies,
6-weight for nymphs

Lines: Weight-forward 6-weight line for both

Flies: Ray Charles, sow bugs, black smoke jumper,
Thor's cripple BWO, caddis and hoppers

Other Essential Gear: Dress for the weather—
it changes often

Don't Forget to Pack: rain jacket is always a must

Because of an abundance of food, Bighorn trout grow at an accelerated rate but seldom live past six years.

The Bighorn River Lodge was our home during our baptism to the river.

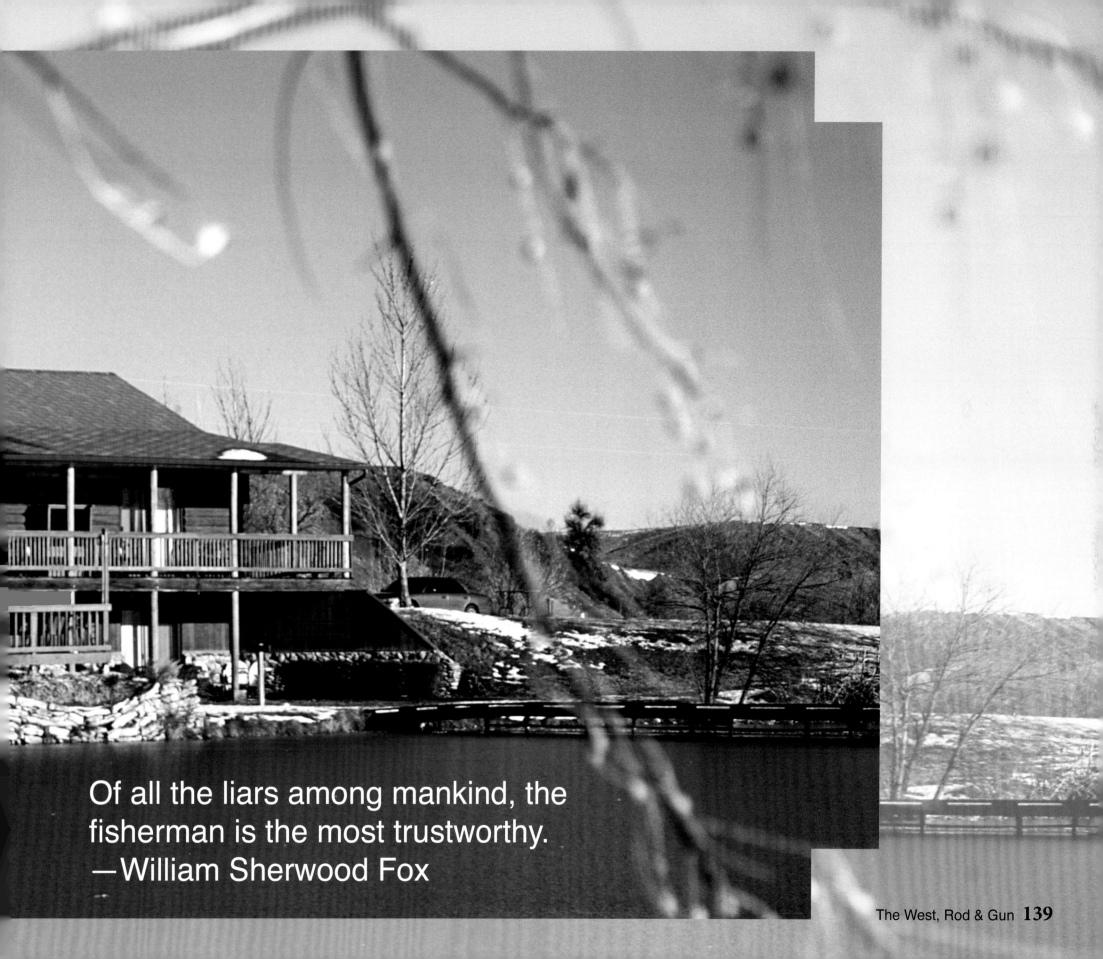

Of all the liars among mankind, the fisherman is the most trustworthy.
—William Sherwood Fox

He is not idle. He is fishing, alone
with himself in dignity and peace. It
seems a very precious thing to me.
—John Steinbeck

3

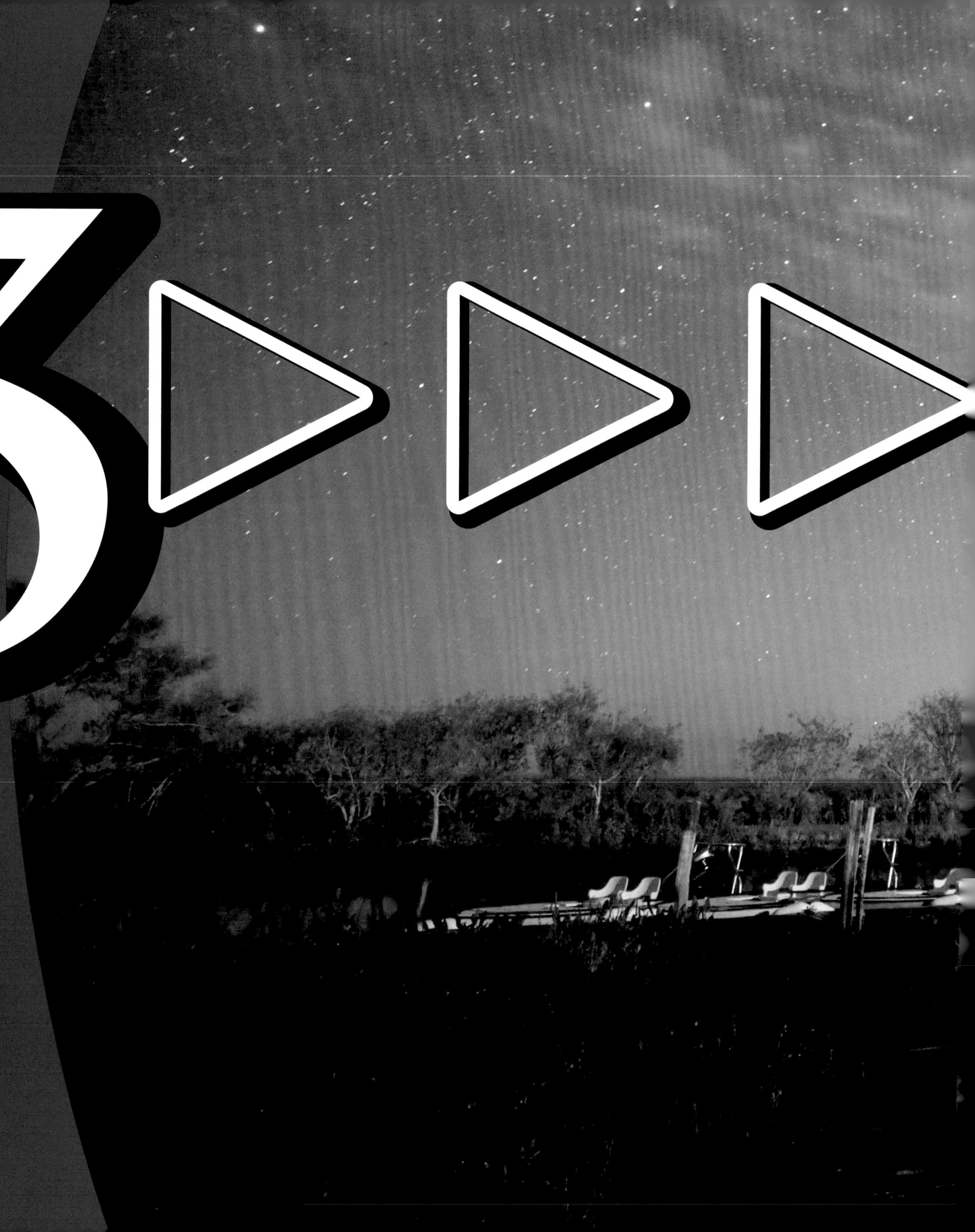

SOUTH AMERICA

A world of fishing on one continent

Fishermen are born honest,
but they get over it. —Ed Zern

Narrow cuts through floating mats of vegetation are sometimes all that connect one dorado pool to another. The endless Ibera Swamp is the second largest wetland in the world, behind only the great Pantanal of Brazil.

Gold Rush

The Hunt
For The Lost Riches
Of The Ibera Swamp

Argentina's seemingly endless Ibera wetlands span some 7,000-square miles, the second largest wetland in the world, behind only Brazil's great Pantanal. It is a labyrinth of rivers, streams, marshes and pools that are the hidden lairs of notorious fly-stealing pirates. Meet the golden dorado, a ruthless fish descended from some malevolent piscatorial order that does not surrender its treasure without penance.

Old friend Matt Connolly and I have come to the end of the Earth to tango with these fish whose beauty belies their vicious nature. Aside from perhaps pike, I do not know of a freshwater fish that so behaves with the savageness of a saltwater species whose survival instincts have been forged in a food chain loaded with predators.

My introduction to the golden dorado was a chance encounter that occurred more than a decade earlier between duck hunts. Our waterfowling lodge sat on the banks of a braided river in the north of the country where the surrounding rice culture made it a haven for scores of waterfowl species. After lunch one day, the lodge manager showed me a fly rod and pointed to the waters below the building and exhausted much of his English in one burst, "Fish there." We had an hour before departing for the afternoon duck hunt; when in Argentina. . . .

Guide Francois Botha is about to release one of the TV stars caught while filming at Pira Lodge, one of the world's most remote fly-fishing destinations, located in the wilds of Argentina.

The 8-weight rod was already rigged with a streamer attached to a wire leader, so I ambled to the bank. But I didn't have a clue for what I was fishing. I began false casting until I dropped the fly into the meandering current about 60 feet from the bank on which I stood. Before I could mend the line, my rod began snapping back and forth like a whip. Suddenly an electric yellow fish was on the end of my line trying to land on the moon.

Three jumps in five seconds and the fish popped off. It was as if I had witnessed an apparition. *What the hell was that?* is all I could think, and there was no one to consult who spoke any English. I felt like the witness to a hit and run with nowhere to report the crime.

Feeling slightly violated by the mugging, I began a naturalist's investigation into the golden dorado and started scheming to make a trip to the country's hot zone for the species. That eventually landed Connolly and me at Pira Lodge, a sprawling compound that blends a gourmet experience with world-class fishing far from civilization. From the lodge, we will launch daily forays into the innumerable channels and hidden bays locked away in the vastness of the marsh.

Our guide is a South African fish gypsy of sorts, Francois Botha, who has become expert at introducing anglers to many of the world's great game fish. He is here now because there's no better place on our planet to be this time of year if you're in need of a fly-fishing fix.

Botha is something of a trout bum who's done well, for he's parlayed his love of fishing into a living sampling the world's best angling. He's a high-energy ambassador for the sport and, like most South Africans I've met, will make his own party if he can't crash one. He takes us through a series of channels and cuts in the marsh en route to some pools where he's previously found good numbers of fish on his prospecting voyages.

Note the setback of the lodge from the river channel. Given that there is almost no grade throughout the vast wetland, the delta routinely floods.

A marsh fire billows in the distance as Matt Connolly is about to connect with yet another golden dorado.

Caiman are ever-present throughout the marsh and feed on everything from birds to fish to the world's largest rodent called the capybara (below), which can grow to upwards of 150 pounds.

In wildness is the
preservation of the world.
—Henry David Thoreau

Few fish protest a hook
like golden dorado, their
cue to take to the skies.

Within 15 minutes of our journey, I am already disorientated to the point where he could have blind-folded me and it would have made little difference to my understanding of our whereabouts. In other words, if Botha suddenly had a widowmaker, Connolly and I would become nothing more than a missing persons cold case. I find that I am extra polite to wilderness guides for, as with a surgeon, it's best to remain on good personal terms.

As we boat to our first dorado pool, we round bends in the channel that are lined with nearly black bear-sized capybaras, a South American beaver of sorts—they're the largest rodents in the world, save for those wandering the maze of Congress. The wetlands also are home to all manner of exotic beasts including a trio of impressive cats: jaguars, puma and ocelots. More-over, there's an abundance of caiman, a South American alligator; anacondas; howler and spider monkeys; and the deadly fer de lance, a pit viper that's part of the "two-stepper" family of snakes owing to how quickly they kill. Then there is an astonishing diversity of bird life, so much, in fact, that you feel as if a large percentage of the world's supply of many of these species must surely reside here.

After the 45-minute wetland tour, we emerge into a series of pools that look like main street for golden dorado. Matt is up and begins false casting as Botha instructs him to shoot his fly to the middle of the channel. About 20 seconds later, there's an eight-pound golden dorado ripping line as it auditions for Cirque du Soleil, spending more time spinning in the air than swimming in the water. In just a few second encounter, there's no mystery left as to why so many anglers journey to this limitless angling paradise. This isn't just one of the world's great freshwater game fish, it is one of the planet's epic sport fish, surrendering nothing to its saltwater brethren.

"What an exquisite fish," says Connolly, basking in the glory of having traveled half-way across the globe to complete the mission of landing a brute of a golden dorado. "I don't know of another fish that looks so much like it was created directly by the hand of God," he says, the encounter moving him to soliloquy as he is sometimes wont to do, part of his charm is his unique ability to do so with or without the benefit of a malt beverage. Connolly, as they say, has forgotten more about fish and fishing than most of the so-called experts. His running Ducks Unlimited for so many years was a clever front for his piscatorial passions; after all, one must have feathers to make flies.

God fish or the work of El Diablo? Depends on what a dorado is doing to your fly at any given moment. As I step to the front of the boat and take my turn plying these waters, I take a shot farther up the channel, undisturbed territory where I'm hoping another fish awaits. Two casts into the pool and the water begins splashing as if a shark is tearing apart of a bonefish, the dorado jumping three times before wrapping around some lily pads and giving me the universal middle fin.

Connolly takes pity on my encounter and surrenders his turn for me to get on the board and land one of the beasts, so I remain at the bow, scanning the waters ahead as Botha poles us into yet another pool. This time I see a fish surface 30 yards ahead, the boil punctuated by the tail of the fish forking out of the water, revealing a dorado of epic proportions. I drop the fly on the last known location of the fish . . . twice. Nothing. I try 10 feet to the left and soon the 8-weight is doubled over and so am I. The rodeo begins and I'm determined not to lose this bronc. After a half-dozen jumps, my first dorado is to the boat, a stunning specimen with teeth that look as if it's been fitted with a piranha smile.

These waters are full of piranha as well, and they're the professional wrestlers of their kind—some pushing seven and eight pounds. The same neighborhoods that are home to the dorado are shared with piranha. Suffice it to say, the weak and infirm are quickly removed from this food chain, no different than a herd of buffalo haunted by lions.

We return to the lodge after a day spent plying the waters of the open river channel, a vastly different golden dorado habitat than is found deeper into the swamp.

Botha releases a tank of a dorado that put a 9-weight rod to the supreme test.

The tattered tails of the region's dorado speak to the savage neighborhood in which they reside.

After hooking several piranha, it becomes clear that they're a highly underrated game fish, for they will take you into the backing and bend a rod with the best fish their size. They're just a public relations campaign away from having their own advocacy organization. Someone ought to trademark "Piranhas Forever" before some law firm grabs the name for their own.

With our piranha curiosity satiated, however, Botha drops the prop and heads to another hidden location—a secret lair because it seems it would be impossible to ever find again. I can't tell if we're simply exploring as we go or if Botha has a destination in mind when he strikes off. Either way, he puts us on fish as if he has a nose for them, so who am I to question his method?

This time we turn into what looks like an old trapper's trail in some Canadian cattail marsh, the kind a pirogue would have difficulty navigating—the same craft Nash Buckingham once referred to as a water-going ashtray. It's a three-foot-wide cut in an otherwise unending floating mat of vegetation that looks as if it could close behind us at any moment like some kind of cosmic-sized Venus fly trap. At a few points along the way, we must stop to pole and pull our way through, feeling more like a portage than a float. Whatever lies at the end of this tortuous journey must be historic, for *who would go to such trouble to get there otherwise*, I think to myself. I hope, anyway. Eventually, we emerge from the sea of reeds and rushes into a five-acre pool.

"This is it guys, get ready," says Botha.

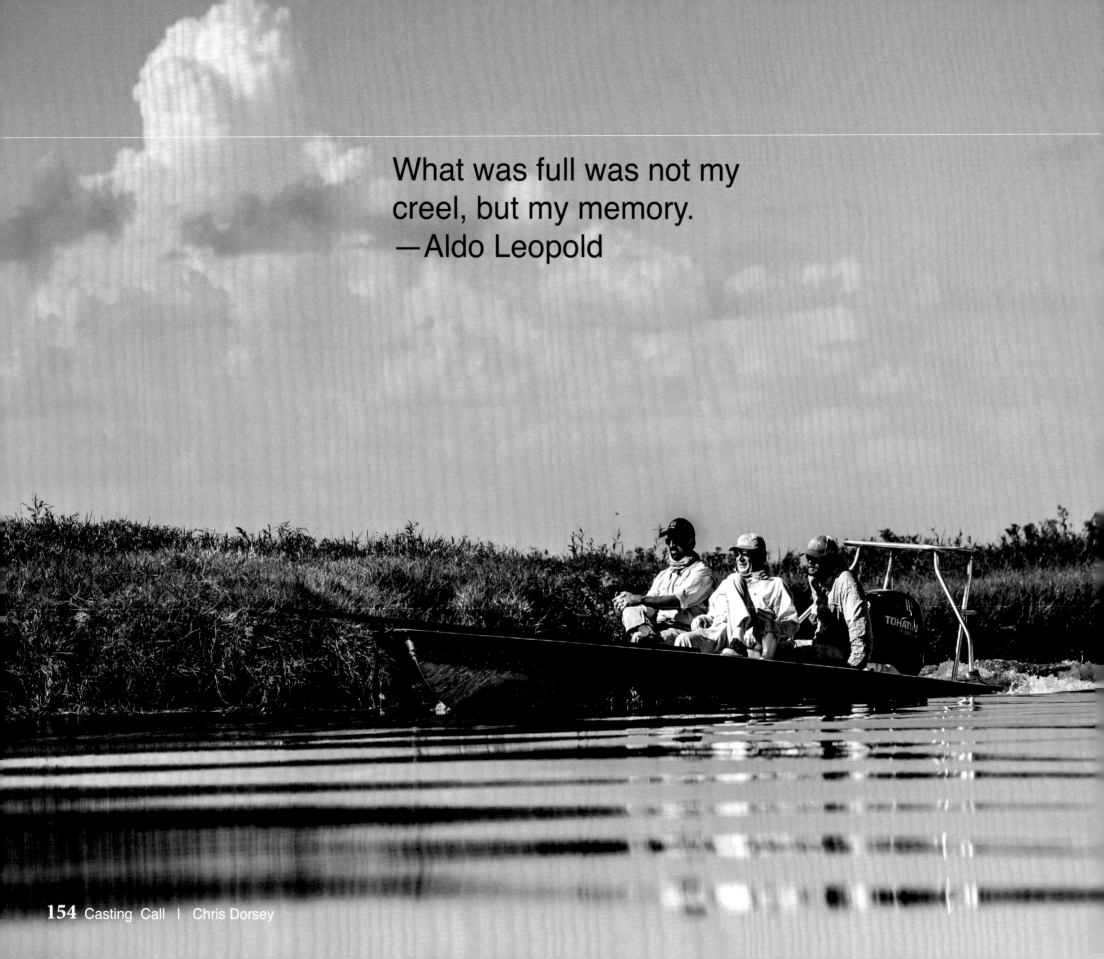

What was full was not my
creel, but my memory.
—Aldo Leopold

No matter the brand, a cold beer after a hot day of fishing is good medicine. . . . maybe two.

I stand and cast to the edge of the reeds, 30 yards to the left. As if a dorado had been waiting for my arrival, it smashes the fly after one strip, trying to kiss the clouds with every jump. Few fish in my experience protest being hooked as much as the golden dorado. Their desire to be free is inspirational, their relationship to a hook being the same as that between cattle and a cattle prod.

Before I can get my fish to the boat, Connolly steps up and sticks a hog of his own, proving that the journey through our own River of Doubt is worthwhile. The stop is rich in golden dorado, numerous fish that act as though they've never seen a human or a fly. When they do, they react like a wolf in a trap. By the end of the afternoon, it's hard not to feel like you've just experienced a piece of the planet no one else has ever seen, as close to a moon landing as Connolly and I will ever get. Angling here is not as much about catching fish as it is being captured by the place, a liquid and plant world so unlike anything else save, perhaps, for the great Okavango Delta of Botswana.

We return to the lodge feeling like the day's adventure alone was enough to justify the whole voyage to the other end of the planet. What more could an angler want?

Nevertheless, we still have a couple more days to explore this seemingly alien environment, so Botha takes us downriver to a much more open channel and river delta, a course perhaps 150 yards wide and much deeper than the marshlands in which we had been fishing. A great part of the appeal of exotic fishing to me is simply answering the question: what lives in these waters? Here, the answer could be almost anything. For instance, a tiger shovel-nose catfish, a flat-headed beast that looks like it was painted by a graffiti artist.

I hook one of the deep water denizens and it's quickly obvious it isn't a dorado, so the initial litany of possibilities run through my head: Capybara? Caiman? Tortoise? Anaconda? Ray? Mermaid?

It isn't until the tractor pull is finished and Botha jumps into the water to hoist the 25-pound cat out of the depths that we see the unique species.

"Look at that fish!" says Botha. "That's quite a unique catch on a fly, my friend."

Our last day, Botha takes Matt and me to yet another of his favorite haunts. After a long journey, we emerge from a screen of reeds to a pool with a series of dead tree stems standing in the midst of the channel, apparently moved there by extraterrestrials because no tree is visible for miles. As we clear the gray, ghostly branches, Connolly sees a fish 20 yards to the left, drops the fly ahead of the dorado and strips it past its nose. It's an irresistible presentation and the 10-pound brute pounds the streamer, taking it with him on umpteen jumps.

Seeing that fish, watching Connolly cast to it and ultimately landing that horse of a dorado becomes a postcard moment of the journey. It's a sight that locks in my mind's eye where it remains to this day. That's the way great trips are remembered, in portraits of the mind—sometimes in one uncontrollable laugh or, if you're lucky, in a kind of epiphany that delivers a yet undiscovered universal truth. After decades of using fish as an excuse to travel, I have my own personal book of fishing revelations: You can't have too many flies when fishing for golden dorado. And bring a GPS, just in case.

What to Bring

Rods: Nine-foot medium-fast action for 7- or 8-weight line

Reels: "Overline" your 7-weight rod with an 8-weight reel

Lines: 300- to 350-grain sinking line—do NOT bring conventional coldwater line

Flies: Big saltwater streamers, No. 2 and 3, in black/red, black/purple; poppers and mice

Other Essential Gear: Polarized lenses and a fishing cap

Don't Forget to Pack: Three-prong adapter for power

A tiger shovel-nose catfish is a surprise visitor when casting to golden dorado, but the 25-pound fish unleashed plenty of fight.

A mug no baitfish wants
to see approaching.

If any gamefish were a candidate to grow wings, it would be the golden dorado that become airborne acrobats at the first hint of being hooked.

In our family, there was no clear line between religion and fly fishing. —Norman Maclean

For the angler-naturalist, the liquid wilderness that is the vast Ibera Swamp is one of the most ecologically rich environments on our planet, resplendent with all manner of reptiles, birds and mammals.

Pira Lodge is a beautifully appointed destination that serves gourmet meals—especially remarkable given its distance from any semblance of civilization.

All fathers pray for their
sons to outfish them.
—Thomas Lynch

Amazon Prime

Sometimes The Best Way To Find Yourself Is To Get Lost—In The Jungle No Less

I am living the experience through the eyes of my twin 14-year-old boys, a childlike adventure that could have been concocted by Zane Grey or Jack London. As the plane fitted with floats careens off the air pockets wafting from the canopy of the Amazon below, I pan to my sons, wondering what must be running through their minds as we're about to touch down in one of the planet's most remote fishing waters, as exotic an environment as exists where the mascots include jaguar, anacondas, macaws and Lord only knows what else.

Our destination is a hidden camp situated on a spit of an island in the midst of the Rio Travessao, a massive waterway home to too many species of fish to count. The location is a mix of *Swiss Family Robinson* and *Gilligan's Island*, a series of huts on stilts with comfortable beds and hot showers . . . and the occasional tarantula doubling as a doormat.

We have come to see about catching the region's giant catfish—Paraiba, red tail and leopard—and any others willing to play along, including peacock bass, wolf fish, bicuda, pacu and the world's largest piranha. The character of this river is very different than the prime peacock waters of the Rio Negro that draws most of the foreign anglers. This is a place for wilderness explorers looking for surprises; there's no way to know what you might reel up out of these murky depths. For 14-year-olds (including my spirit), solving the mystery of what lurks beneath will contain much of the intrigue of this journey. That and watching the boys live their River Monsters dreams, potentially taming creatures larger than themselves.

My wife Amy and I situate in our hut while the twins have one of their own. After two days of travel to get here, the boys are as eager to explore as a pair of birds dogs fresh out of the kennel. Nate and I load up a mix of what look like stout saltwater spin rods and reels as well as a nine-weight fly rod. We're armed with all manner of nasty lures that look like they're built to attract some kind of prehistoric beasts leftover in these forbidden waters. Amy and Luke have similar rigs and hop in a boat of their own for the day. We'll see them again late in the afternoon when the camp will undoubtedly be abuzz with plenty of fish tales, some of them perhaps even bearing a resemblance to truth.

Sunset over the Amazon brings enthusiasm for what tomorrow will bring. Thousands of fish species live in these waters and we want to catch every one of them.

As a parent, you try not to generalize too much about your kids because their passions for sports and pastimes often changes quickly, but Nate has long had a fascination with fishing and fish in general. About five years ago, his love of all things mechanical morphed into an obsession with catching fish. His epiphany brought a simple clarity to his existence with these basic questions forever in need of answering: What fish live here and how do I get them to bite?

This trip is much about Nate and unleashing his piscatorial passions in waters where seemingly catching anything is possible. Our shoulder-height aboriginal guide, perhaps 30-something—though it's tough to tell with this tribe—steers our boat to the mouth of a small creek feeding into the main channel of the river. These confluences are fishy the world over, but unlike finding a brown or rainbow on the Big Hole or the Madison, we're not altogether certain what might lie beneath the surface here.

`The guide hands us each rods, points to the calm waters under some overhanging vegetation and directs simply, "Cast there."

Nate flips his wooden lure with all manner of hooks and spinning parts exactly where instructed. The lure looks like a blender working its way across the surface until a peacock bass interrupts the retrieve and begins cartwheeling through the air as if it's being electrocuted. Streaks of yellow and green shoot into the sky as the fish seems utterly terrorized by the prospect of being hooked. It's Nate's baptism to these waters and a sturdy seven-pound fish at that, a species that was breakdancing before it was cool.

We take turns catching these gamers, coming to understand what all the hype is about with peacocks. Simply, they are a species that calls into question their relationship to gravity, as if they may have evolved as much from birds as anything aquatic. Despite the common name, they're not closely related to bass at all, but rather are *cichlids*, which few know is Latin for ass kicker. While they're found in far greater abundance in the Rio Negro and other Amazon tributaries, there are enough of them here that they provide one of the main courses of a very diverse menu, which is the unique appeal of this river.

A green vine snake slithers along the
bank as we cast for peacock bass.

Nate's first Amazon peacock brings plenty of smiles and a thirst for more. While the Rio Negro holds far more peacocks, the Rio Travessao's charm is the diversity of fish species that inhabit these waters from the giant Paraiba, redtail and leopard catfish to wolf fish, pacu and the world's largest piranhas.

A kayak and a fly rod—and plenty of ambition—were all that Nate needed to hook his first peacocks on a fly.

We return to camp, and Amy and Luke greeting us with Cheshire cat grins on their faces, owing to having met peacocks of their own. We chug cold beers—Amy and I, that is—on the banks of the river below camp. For a moment, I muse how far we are from a small trout stream that she and I once fished in the Ozarks when we were courting lo those many years ago. Before kids, mortgages, responsibilities and the like. There's something about staring at a river with a beer in your hand that raises the muse. Should it not respond, add more beer.

What will the currents of time bring the twins? Health, wealth and wisdom—or something else? A great love—or heartache? How much time will we have together? Do we have miles to go before we sleep, as Frost suggested? Or will the trail end before we know it? What I do know is that we could not be spending our time together better, and I'm grateful for the moment. As the great bard of rivers, Sparse Grey Hackle cautioned, "The trout don't rise in Greenwood Cemetery."

The next morning Luke and I head to a large, deep pool in the river, maybe 30 minutes upriver. We stop and anchor to a long, naked tree stem that has fallen from the bank and juts into the river like a street lamp knocked askew. Our guide puts chunks of paku on baseball-sized treble hooks and hands the rebar like rods to us to begin casting in the midst of the current, a two-pound lead sinker attached to the rig. Either we are fishing for Volkswagens or there are fish down there for which we should have brought a rifle.

The 60-pound redtail catfish is one of the prized species of the Rio Travessao, for their combined heft and fight make them as formidable as a hernia.

Then we wait. And wait some more, occasionally recasting to get the bait back into the hole the guide is convinced will produce a fish. Just as we're about to leave, my rod slams to the rim of the boat. The question is, what is on the end of my line? Paraiba? Red tail? No, a leopard catfish, a 25-pound specimen with a dark brown body that looks as if someone used chicken wire as a stencil to create the intricate pattern on its skin. I hoist the beast to the boat after a 15-minute fight, the final cranks of the reel feel like the last turns opening a sardine can. It's a remarkably strong fighter that has no interest in reaching the surface, seemingly as light-shy as a vampire.

With our catfish fight over, Luke and I head farther upriver to a shallow bay off the bank in a section where the flowage is more than a half-mile wide. Luke begins flipping his topwater lure toward shore, bringing it back as fast as he can reel. Two casts in, the lure is smashed by a peacock, the kind of violent strike that is the hallmark of the species, which is its great attraction to anglers. He catches several more peacocks before we move farther to find a fresh pool of undisturbed fish.

This time, we wind our way into a tributary, the over-hanging branches giving it the feel of some obscured waterway you'd see in a low-budget horror flick leading to a lost tribe of cannibals. Overhead macaws fly kite-like, squawking their protest at our intrusion. A wild muscovy duck flies head of us, as if leading the way upriver. We're not sure where we're heading but reckon that there must be a good reason for detouring so far off the main channel.

After the half-hour run, we pull to the edge of a 60-yard-wide pool and drop anchor. It feels as if we have a reservation, the guide doesn't hesitate when he reaches the hole. In case you're wondering, they don't use electronics. There are no fish finders or sonar, no GPS or the like. The tribes who live in this bioreserve have simply been fishing these waters for generations, discovering the addresses of various fish species by learning from their elders and knocking on watery doors for decades.

Peacock bass don't so much take a fly as they savage it. Cast to cover, strip fast and get ready for a rodeo.

With my hook baited again, I pitch the rig into the pool as advised by the guide. There isn't a great deal of conversation given the language barrier but there is a clear understanding of *what* to do and *when*. The *why* is a bit murky, however. Nevertheless, we cast on blind faith and wait to see what is delivered. This time, I get another hard pull on my line, the rod bouncing up and down as something hefty and testy is making a run with my hook. I fight back, bending the stout rod in half and pumping the reel like some kind of blue water behemoth is at the end of the line. Instead, I pull up an utterly prehistoric looking wolf fish, a toothy, semi-evolved leftover from the primordial ooze. We snap a few photos and I'm about to release it when the guide intervenes.

"No, no, no . . . lunch . . . we eat for lunch."

I've enjoyed shore lunches from the wilds of Alaska to Quebec salmon rivers but I had the feeling this one was about to be a bit different. We wind our boat back to the main channel of the river and find an open sandy beach to pull in and build a fire. Soon the fish is scaled and steaming in banana leaves, their preparation as matter-of-fact as a hotdog on a grill. When it comes to hunger, mankind has been adept at converting all manner of wild protein into lunch or dinner since the arrival of early man to these waters.

My guide hoists a small cooler out of the back of the boat with seasoning and a sweet chutney like fruit sauce, the combination making for some of the best fish I've ever eaten—anywhere. The flesh of the wolf fish is almost halibut or barramundi like, a dense yet moist white meat. Lunch wraps with a nap on hammocks that are quickly strung between trees to keep you above any slithering visitors that might arrive from beneath the ever-present leaf litter. It's a mid-day ritual that is its own variation on *siesta*.

Float planes arriving from Manaus are the only practical way into camp located on a tiny island in the midst of the Rio Travessao's sprawling river delta.

Reaching prime catfish lairs requires negotiating an extensive rapids where the sure-footed guides walk the boats to the promised waters.

South America, Amazon Prime 173

It's not uncommon to motor an hour or two to reach the river's most productive pools. The question is: what do you want to catch? Once the guides determine that, they then head to the last known address of that species.

Another full day of exploring, catching and feasting on the books, it's Amy's and my turn to fish together. We are eager to find the famed red tail catfish of the region, the 50-plus pound giants with their white underbellies, dark backs and striking red tails.

"If you really want to catch them," says Wellington, the camp manager, "we'll need to make a long run upriver."

"What's a couple of hours given how far we've already come?" I say with a smile. Loosely translated, *of course we want to catch them, why would you even ask?* I think to myself.

We head far upriver, getting a look at this amazing environment with its never ending jungle, diverse bird life, caiman along the bank and densely woven vegetation lining the whole of the waterway. About the time we are wondering if our passports are still valid here, our guide slows the full throttle of the motor to ease to the end of a large pool, rigs up a massive treble hook and points to where we are to shotput the weighted bait. Amy does just that and within a couple of minutes her rod is contorting and so is she, giggling with the nervous anticipation of what, exactly, might be fighting on the other end of the line.

Maybe 20 minutes pass and the basketball sized head of a red tail catfish finally emerges from the depths, tipping the boat as our guide hoists it out of the water. My bride emits a kind of giggle—which the twins dubbed the "figgle,"

fish plus giggle—each time she catches a fish, it's an involuntary reaction to getting hooked. The intensity of the figgle is directly proportional to the size of the fish, so it's in overdrive as this buffalo of a catfish breaks the surface.

Pictures taken, fish released and happy wife. Check. My turn to see if I can do the same. As if they cued the twin to Amy's fish, I hook a red tail almost instantly after she completes her catch and release process. The rodeo begins anew, the incredibly strong cat feels like I'm reeling in cinder blocks—several of them. This isn't finesse fishing, to be sure, but there is something wholly satisfying about subduing a heavyweight leviathan in a game of tug of war as old as Jonah and the Whale.

As family vacations go, we'll likely never come to appreciate any wilderness as much as we did the Amazon and its people. With much of the planet having succumbed to electronics and conveniences that replace connections, it's nice to know a piece of our world has remained unchanged. At the end of the day, so have we. Sometimes we must remind ourselves of that and disconnect from one world to plug into one another.

Caiman are found throughout the Amazon and may grow to 10 feet or longer.

Amy's super-sized redtail was caught after a two hour run upriver. The guides knew exactly where to find the redtails and pulled into a large calm pool in the river as though they had made reservations.

The delightful crew of our Swiss Family Robinson jungle camp
made our family experience that much more unforgettable.

Nate hooks into an as yet unknown
leviathan as Luke awaits his own tug.
Catfish? Wolffish? Lord only knows. . . .

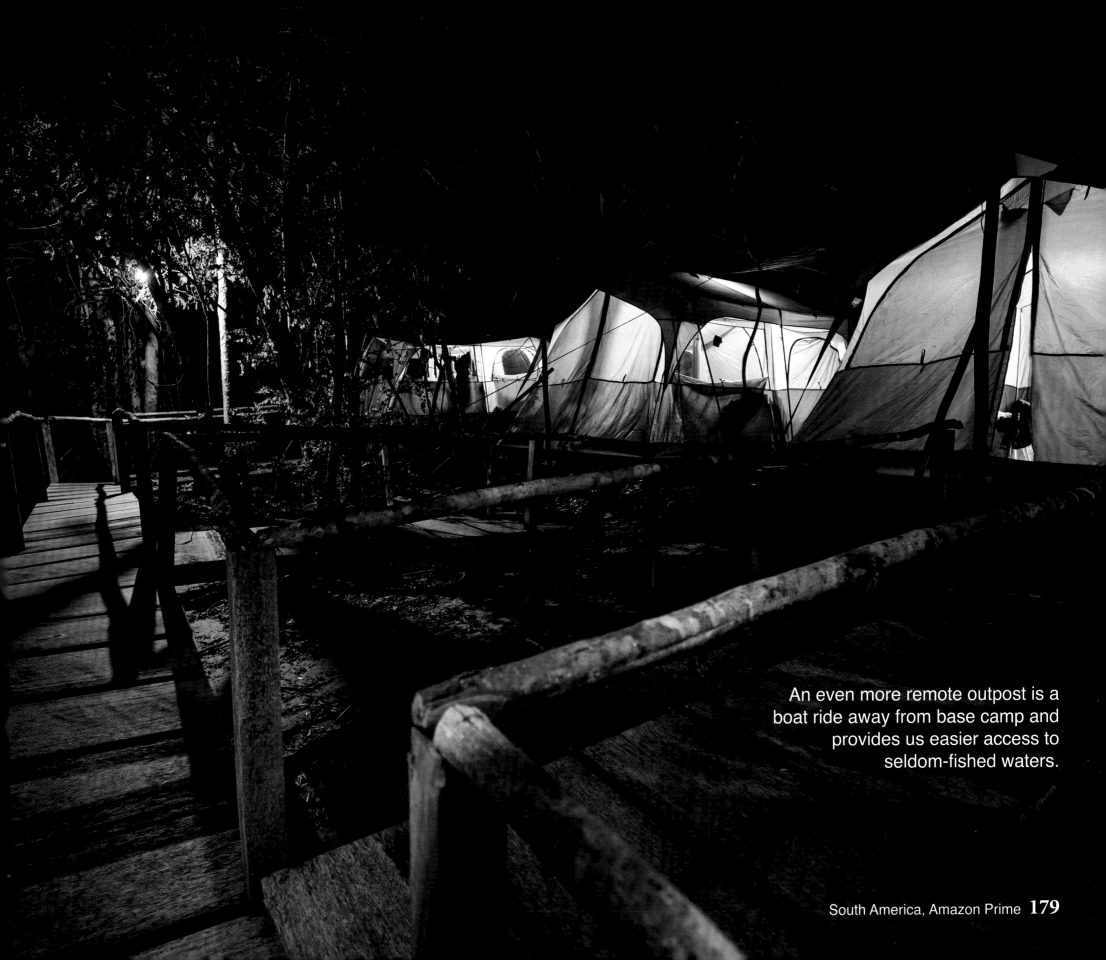

An even more remote outpost is a boat ride away from base camp and provides us easier access to seldom-fished waters.

Luke's first peacock of the foray
turned the calm pool in which we
were fishing into a blender as
the fish savaged his fly.

A shore lunch of wolffish was among the best fish I've ever eaten: a delicious flaky white meat cooked over an open fire and served on banana leaves.

The lonely waters of Patagonia deliver epic fishing for both browns and rainbows.

Passing The Time

Drifting The Rivers Of Patagonia Is A Return To Montana Of The 1940s

A s we drive the dirt track, bouncing our way ever closer to the river lined with giraffe-tall poplars glowing lemon in the Patagonian sun, it feels like we are about to float a river that starts somewhere in Montana or Colorado before winding its way to the bottom of South America. As we reach the put-in, cattle watch us like buffalo might a lion, trying to discern if we are delivering hay for them or are about to take them to the abattoir.

Instead, we are met at the river by Kevin Tiemersma, the managing partner of Tipiliuke Lodge, a destination that has become an irresistible lure for many hunters and anglers looking to immerse themselves in all things Patagonian sporting. Tiemersma is never far from a smile and revels in showing his home waters to visitors that travel the world chasing rumors of epic browns in this land of the lost angler. He introduces me to Federico "Fede" Obejero, a 30-something recovering attorney turned fishing guide.

Why travel to the end of the Earth to catch trout? This is why.

Host Kevin Tiemersma trains
one of the Chimehuin giants.

t's April and the river looks like a perfect replica of the Big Hole in early October. There isn't a cloud anywhere and the temperatures are in the mid-60s, pretty close to a perfect day for what we are about to do. Our mission is to separate the river from some
of its heftiest trout. And I am non-denominational, happy to catch either browns or rainbows. I am armed with a 5-weight, a
pocket full of dries and an eagerness to see what all the fuss is about when it comes to Patagonian angling.

I begin training my line and greasing my elbow for the work ahead with a series of false casts as Fede rows us across the
75-yard span of the river, to a nearby pocket that looks particularly fishy. I drop my fly under a willow bush, looking like a piece of cotton
just hit the water. In the same instant that it meets the water, a 10-inch brown mugs it, turning in a splash and diving for the depths below.
After having just come off a bonefishing foray where I was casting an 8-weight against an eternal wind, the 5-weight feels like I am fishing
with a car antennae, experiencing every ounce of fight the fish delivers.

We are adrift on a nine-mile stretch of the Chimehuin River, one of two famous trout waters that split the 50,000 acres of Tipiliuke.
The other is the much smaller Quilquihue—in total there are 17 miles of private waters here and Lord only knows how many trout per
river mile.

We concentrate our efforts in a series of side pools along the bank, tucked away from the main force of the river's meandering current. It flows like a prairie river, something akin to the Big Hole below Melrose. Maybe 50 yards downriver from my first trout, I tap the surface with two quick- tease casts before letting the fly rest on the third. It proves the charm as another brown, perhaps a bit better than the first, gulps the fly and decides to make a run downriver, using his body as a sail to harness the current, punching deceptively above its weight class.

We fish for a couple of hours and land a mix of browns and rainbows, but nothing over 14 inches. Still, a fish on a dry is worth three below the surface in my book, but I'm not above trying a streamer to see if I can find one of the spotted hogs for which the Chimehuin is so famous. Some of those fish reach legendary proportions, the river occasionally producing browns approaching 30 inches, a key part of the draw to fishing this piece of Patagonia.

With plenty of action from my morning float, I return to the lodge, a two-story structure that looks like a beautifully restored ranch house tucked inside a planted—and enchanted—forest of evergreens. It's a chlorophyll oasis of sorts, for the rest of the ranch is comprised of rolling dry grass steppes where the wind talks to itself in blustery conversations. Immediately surrounding the lodge is a sprawling lawn where a table is set for lunch and wafts of aroma from grilling meats lead us in like lions to a fresh kill.

Herds of wild stags roam the hills above the Chimehuin River. The animals were introduced more than a century ago and have thrived since.

If it's dry-fly action you seek,
Tipiliuke is the place for you.

Fall in Patagonia is often temperate
and the staff at Tipiliuke seize every
opportunity to remain outdoors.

A diverse menu of locally grown vegetables, salads and meats fuels long days of fishing and hunting.

t would be a form of gastronomic torture to be a vegetarian here, for each meal is a carnivore's celebration of sausages, chops and loins where it's possible to eat your way into a coma if you're not careful. And if you fall victim to the medium rare orgy, there's always the possibility of a nap if you'd rather ruminate like a lumpy snake for a bit before returning to the river.

Joining the lunch table is a trio of Americans who spent the morning chasing California quail behind guide Adrian Cataldi and his ace pointer, Deuce. The quail were introduced a century ago and have found the Patagonian terrain, cover and temperatures (and relative lack of predators) to their liking, becoming prolific across much of the ranch. Another hunter who spent the morning chasing snipe joins us as well along with a man in search of one of the ranch's stags. Of all the sporting retreats I've visited over 30 years of avoiding honest work, Tipiliuke offers arguably the most eclectic menu of pursuits.

The ranch has an interesting past as well. The property was purchased in 1909 by Jacques de Larminat, a Frenchman who had two brothers who came to help him establish a sheep operation far from the impending threats of war in Europe. When the first World War broke out, however, all three brothers went to fight but only Jacques survived to return to continue developing the ranch. The property sits in the shadow of the enormous snow-covered Lanin Peak, a 12,000-foot volcano that towers outrageously from the steppe like some alien marker constructed to direct landing space craft.

Wind-swept steppes are the hallmark of the Patagonian landscape.

A generous mix of rainbows and browns in the 12 to 16 inch range greeted us but the river offers plenty of fish in excess of 20-inches.

Satiated by more meat than I've ever consumed at one sitting, I return to the river if for no other reason than to stop eating. I'm in search of a beastly brown and have come ready for a tussle, which also might provide the benefit of helping burn off some of my caloric overdose.

This beautifully braided and wild river is simply as inviting a piece of trout stream as I've ever seen in my journey to fish the planet's best waters. The purity of catching fish on top—without the plumbing of indicators, droppers and bang-yourself-in-the-back-of-the-head weights—is altogether refreshing. It's a reminder of what the American West must have been like a half-century ago, before dams, channelization and center-pivot irrigation forever altered most of our trout fisheries . . . and before *A River Runs Through It* became *A Realtor Runs Through It*.

Fede is trying to find a big trout willing to accept my Parachute Adams, for he seems reticent to stoop below the surface with a streamer or some other sacrilege. After hooking umpteen browns and rainbows in the 10- to 13-inch range, however, I'm hoping Fede will surrender his pride without me having to reveal myself a Philistine and suggest we switch to a streamer. I'm channeling vibes that it would be ok to forgo the dries just for the drug of a big tug. He's not having it.

He sends back a strong, unspoken message that I loosely translate to, *Sorry, Gringo, I will not defile myself or this boat with a streamer . . . no matter how many not-so-subtle hints you drop.*

I smile and focus on enjoying a glorious day in Patagonia and a river bent on offering up scores of fish willing to eat on top, so while none were the rod-benders whose pictures are floating throughout the fishing cybersphere, I am content with the bounty provided until Tipiliuke and I meet again.

And it can't be soon enough—with a streamer in my pocket.

What to Bring

Rods and Reels: Bring a 4-weight and a 6-weight

Lines: Usually floating lines—the big guys like to be deep, though

Flies: Classic Montana fly box is ideal with assorted dry flies, nymphs and streamers

Other Essential Gear: Wading shoes with felt soles

Don't Forget to Pack: An appetite

In Argentina,
most meals are
festivals of meat,
a carnivore's
delight.

Birds eye view of Tipiliuke
shrouded in morning fog, with
12,000-foot Lanin Peak towering
in the distance.

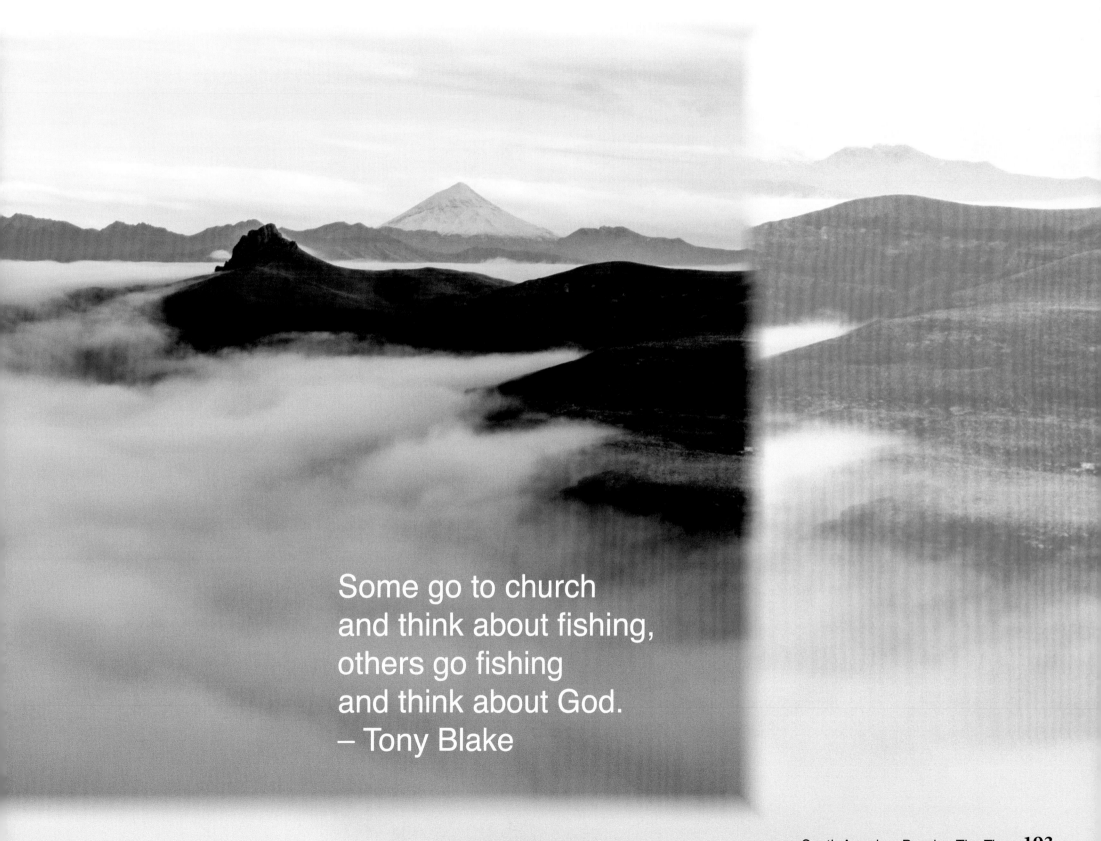

Some go to church
and think about fishing,
others go fishing
and think about God.
– Tony Blake

The lodge at Tipiliuke is surrounded by a man-made forest of sorts, for every tree and shrub was introduced to this grassland region.

Grass-fed Argentinian beef
is among the most flavorful
in the world.

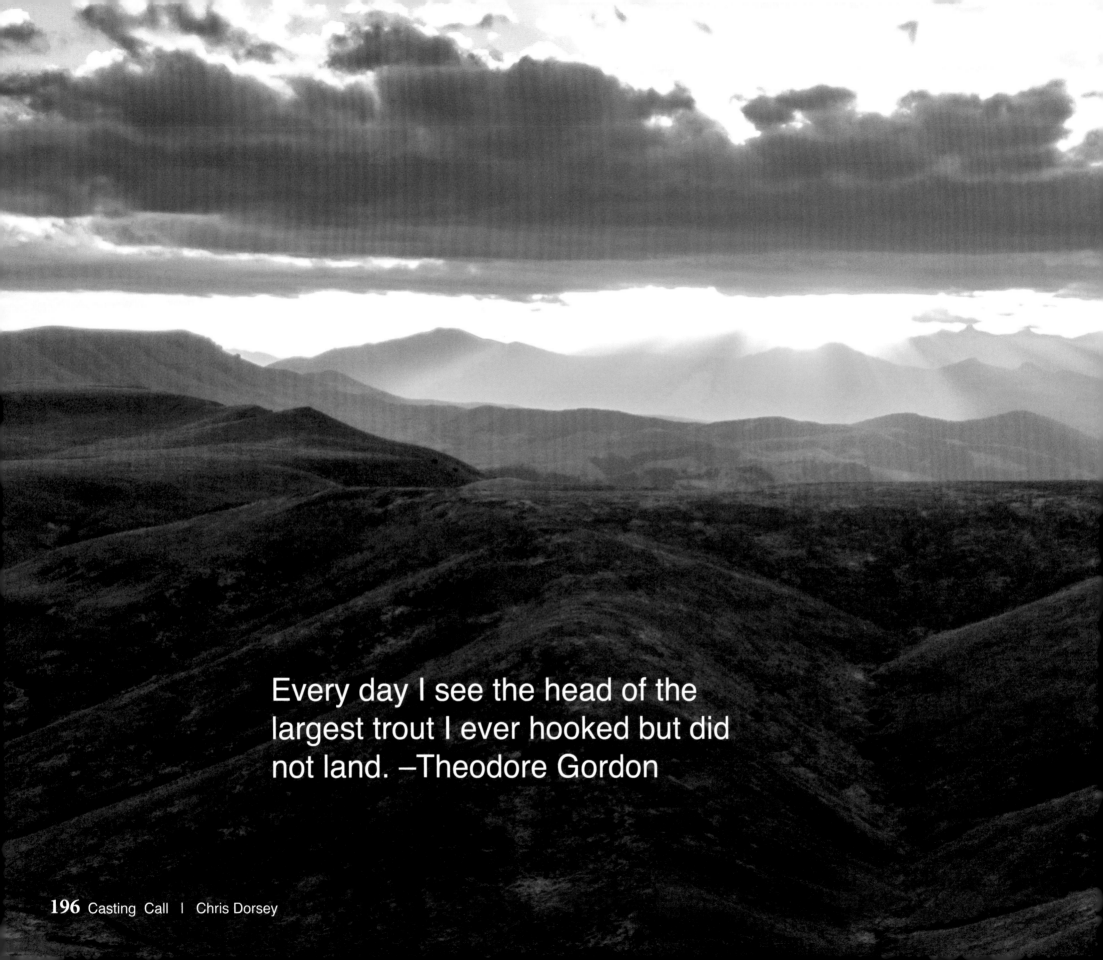

Every day I see the head of the largest trout I ever hooked but did not land. –Theodore Gordon

Patagonia is a land that
time forgot, one of the lonliest
pieces of our planet...just the way
an angler likes it.

Matt Connolly can't resist an early cast for the Rio Negro's legendary peacocks.

A good gamefish is too valuable to be caught only once. The fish you release is your gift to another angler.
—Lee Wulff

Rumble In The Jungle
A Tug-Of-War With The Amazon's Legendary Peacock Bass

The fly line dangles in my grip like a torn parachute cord ripped at 10,000 feet. A volunteer knot (the kind I'm especially gifted at tying) formed around my reel handle in the midst of a run by the biggest peacock bass I've encountered in three days of blind casting to the tea-colored waters of Brazil's Rio Negro. The beast jumped twice before heading for deep water, pulling a small bird's nest of line from the deck of the bass boat to my reel, providing all the leverage necessary for the fish to pop the hook before I could shake the knot loose.

I sit in the boat in a postpartum hangover, wondering if I'll ever encounter another fish of such scale. After three days of double-hauling until my hands are bleeding and numb, I'm fighting the pessimist in me who is saying, simply, *You picked a helluva time to wiff on a fish.*

There's no wasting time getting from one honey hole to another.

Matt Connolly has plenty of reason to smile after landing this monster.

Was the fish at least 15 pounds? No question. Could it have been 20 pounds? Without a doubt. Might it have topped the current world record of 27 pounds? Who knows? This is, after all, a fish tale that isn't burdened by the necessity of proof. Anyone suggesting that size doesn't matter is, well, likely a communist.

My return to the Amazon basin has been 15 years in the making. As a college student I explored Ecuador's Rio Napo by houseboat, stopping occasionally to catch enough piranhas for jungle fish fries. They didn't differ appreciably from the Canadian version where walleye and tartar sauce meet, taking you to heaven one mouthful at a time.

As our charter flight from the jungle city of Manaus descends to a compound that appears to be a small village tucked into the jungle, we get a hint of the enormity of the rainforest whose tightly woven canopy—at least from our perch several thousand feet in the air—resembles the world's supply of broccoli. Few place names conjure a greater sense of mystery than the Amazon, a land both foreboding and exhilarating on the order of Alaska or the Serengeti.

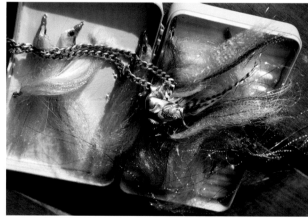

Arrive armed with plenty of flies for the bass will savage them in a hurry.

My inaugural trip to the Amazon was rich in both big fish and abundant numbers of them.

oining me for the peacock hunt are friends Joe Coogan and Matt Connolly. Coogan's a recovering African professional hunter turned writer and Connolly is the retired chief of Ducks Unlimited. Both are inveterate bass anglers who, like me, have longed to confirm the rumors of the Rio Negro's abundance of legendary peacocks.

The Negro is one of the largest arteries feeding the Amazon and its labyrinth of endless side channels and oxbows are a hint of what the Mississippi and Missouri must have looked like before there was an Army Corps of Engineers and an arrogance to think we could tame Mother Nature on a continental scale. The river is a peacock bass paradise, rife with all manner of pools and structure to support both the bass and a cast of other fish that provide local subsistence hand-liners and visiting sport fishermen with ample reason to fly 5,000 miles to ply its waters.

Of the roughly 20 subspecies of peacock bass (and they're not bass at all, but rather are members of a family of fish called *cichlids*), there are three primary varieties found in the waters around the Rio Negro Lodge. The most common is the butterfly pavon (also referred to as the *mariposa* peacock). This subspecies runs between two and four pounds. Another common subspecies is the speckled pavon (sometimes called the *tiger* peacock). This strain is the hardest fighting of all the peacocks and the world record peacock was a speckled variety. Lastly, the peacock pavon is yet another subspecies that also can grow upwards of 20 pounds and is distinguished by three distinctive bars running vertically across the fish.

Our destination is an impossibly large and luxuriant outpost in the middle of the jungle. The lodge and private villas are carved into the forest while an impressive fleet of new bass boats line the river's shoreline below the lodge. Adjacent to a dock that serves as the departure point for anglers each day, sits a pair of float planes that are used to ferry anglers to and from remote lakes and hidden sections of the river throughout this stretch of Amazonas. The extent of the infrastructure is especially astounding when one considers just how far removed the lodge is from any sense of civilization and supply chains.

The cozy confines inside the Rio Negro Lodge brought a constant reminder of why we were here...to catch fish as big as those in the tank.

How animated and
beautiful a pool becomes
when a fighting fish surges to
its surface to do or die!
–Gordon MacQuarrie

The arsenal before the battles begin. Cast, strip for all you're worth and hold on for dear life.

The Forest Primeval

Our guide, a 30-something local named Francival, turns our boat toward a shallow lagoon surrounded by a stand of primitive palm trees with row upon row of vicious spikes running the length of their porcupine-like stems. The plants look as if they're from another epoch, descendants of the trees that could have provided T-rex with the cover necessary to ambush lesser dinosaurs.

Given the Jurassic setting, it wasn't clear what might be pulling at our flies as we ripped them through the still backwaters. Connolly was the first to find out as he no sooner began to strip his green and yellow Deceiver than a flash of parrot green smashed the fly, the fish making a run along the bank of the river. Before Connolly could bring in his butterfly peacock, my streamer elicits a similar strike. Both fish are less than five pounds, but the hallmark of these so-called bass is the larger than life-size fight they offer anglers.

Almost as fast as we could get the flies back into the water, we spotted a small school of the peacocks hovering around the shallows that were pock-marked with fish beds that resembled so many bluegill spawning areas back home. The first fly to hit the water drew a crowd of the aggressive fish, and my followup cast picked up one of the stragglers as we, again, were both hooked up nearly as fast as we could get the fly out.

The afternoon yielded some 30 fish in all, and it's not uncommon for fly fishers to catch more fish than bait casters, but conventional tackle still accounts for more large fish. In five days of fly fishing, the two of us each boated some 150 fish; there are logs revealing that during particularly successful weeks, some fly anglers have boated that many fish in a single day. For sure, a fly fisher surrenders little to his bait-casting brethren when it comes to catching peacocks. In fact, the three fly fishers in our party of a dozen anglers caught 10 to 1 the number of fish hooked by conventional tackle anglers.

After catching an abundance of smallish fish, however, every angler wants to hook into one of the double-digit brutes that can turn a calm backwater into a piscatorial car wash as fast as you can set a hook. Every evening back at the lodge, anglers and guides converge to share stories from the day's foray. Each guide is provided a digital camera to separate fact from fiction, so at the end of the day our ritual is to stand around a computer screen where the images run as a slide show bringing a mix of pride and envy washed down with beer. Such is angling in the digital age.

The Hunt for Big Fish

H en peacocks have an interesting habit of collecting their fry in their mouths when they sense their offspring are in danger. When spooked, the fry will bunch up into a soft ball-sized school. The female, then, will engulf the fry in her catcher's mitt of a mouth, holding the fish there for protection until the danger has passed. When the female releases the fry, a small pod of bubbles will burst on the surface. Savvy guides know that this is an invitation to catch a trophy-sized peacock.

For veteran fly fisher and saltwater angling guide Rufus Wakeman, the third day of his stay at Rio Negro presented the opportunity to drop his fly into the midst of these bubbles, thus inducing a strike from the female that views the intruding fly as a threat to her fry. His ability to make a long cast when the bubble opportunity presented itself allowed him to boat a 15-pound behemoth, still a fish four pounds smaller than his personal record taken during one of his seven previous trips to Rio Negro Lodge.

For Coogan, a combination of a bait caster and Woodchopper lure proved an effective one-two punch to hook a 13-pounder on the first day of his excursion, the largest fish he would boat in a week of angling. For the fly-fishing firm of Connolly and Dorsey, however, such a fish still seems ambitious as the biggest fish to this point is something less than six pounds.

"How 'bout we fish where you take your friends," I query to Francival who smiles politely at my attempt at humor. He nods and heads across the vast breadth of the Rio Negro as he winds our way through a maze of narrow backwater channels where mahogany trees tower above us, providing plenty of perches for the region's plethora of bird life: toucans, macaws, parrots, harpy eagles and countless other fowl.

Peacocks come in a mix of sizes and color patterns but they are not in the bass family.

Scores of inlets and tributaries of the Rio Negro house untold numbers of peacock bass with very little fishing pressure.

Connolly prepares to river dance as the woody vegetation surrounding this pool is prime ambush country for peacocks.

We emerge out of the meandering river corridor into a football field-sized lagoon resplendent with the kind of structure that we've heretofore found to hold the lion's share of fish. *Apparently, all we had to do was ask*, I think to myself. We round a point jutting into the pool and, as we do so, Francival points to an open stretch of water away from shoreline brush. I cast 60 feet in the direction Francival points, strip once, strip twice . . . *bam!* . . . a peacock slams the fly and immediately runs to deeper water across the lagoon.

With most of my fly line out and the fish headed for cover, I decide to try and turn the fish by cupping the reel ever-so-gently, trying not to pop the hook in the process. Just as I do, it erupts out of the water in a violent pirouette that reveals a double-digit fish. I play the river monster off the reel for another 10 minutes, the peacock jumping four more times before Francival finally slips the net under it. It turns out to be 12 pounds of peacock and, given the fight of this specimen, I wonder if I should have brought a rifle for backup.

I surrender the bow of the boat to Connolly who is eager to snap his string of single-digit catches. Soon he is fighting a three-pound butterfly, but the fish serves more as an interruption than a welcomed catch. After shaking the diminutive bass from his line, Connolly's strip is interrupted by a savage burst that bends his rod in a pulsing 90-degree angle. The 10-pound peacock bursts out of the water in a protest that is the signature of trophy peacocks from Venezuela to the Amazon. It's the punctuation to an unforgettable rumble in the jungle, for the punch of a peacock is as memorable as an Ali left hook. 🌑

What to Bring

Rods and Reels: Nine-foot 9-weight

Lines: Sinking lines

Flies: Six-inch streamers in red/yellow, olive/white, orange/black. Big Deceivers, bunnies, Zonkers and Clouser Minnows all take fish

Other Essential Gear: Be ready for sun and rain

Don't Forget to Pack: Power adapter

While fly anglers caught more fish on average during our trip than conventional tackle fishermen, the wood-chopper chuckers landed the biggest fish.

The tannin waters of the Rio Negro explain the river's name. Despite the jungle environs, there were few mosquitoes to interrupt our fishing pleasure.

THE FLATS

Double haul adventures in Listerine waters

213

Few sights are as welcomed on the flats as a tailing bonefish.

Ultimate Bone Yards
Wading With The Ghosts Of Gil Drake At Deep Water's Bonefish Paradise

Growing up in the heartland, I used to cast to available walleye, bass and trout—sometimes yanking them through the ice like a lubricated Neanderthal. Thus, the notion of wading barefoot in the natural spa of a Caribbean flat struck me as an activity reserved for privileged free spirits. They're easy to recognize: perpetual tans and sun-bleached locks, living a sort of perpetual Margaritaville existence.

They sometimes sport bonefish tattoos that grow with age—or arousal. Many I have met seem to spend more time thinking and talking about the flats than they do on them. Their personal highlight reels feature fish. They grow long beards, bathe occasionally (wading a flat passes for hygiene in these circles) and when they gather for happy hour they are often compelled by their kind to share a metaphysic epiphany born on a flat. They do this while staring west in anticipation of the green flash, forever pondering whether the phenomenon is physical or psychedelic. I'm pretty sure that had I grown up on a warmwater coast, I would have been one of them.

Come January and February, with a foot of snow on the ground and howling winds outside, tuning into television shows where the water looks like something to be gargled, feels like some kind of tease, an angler's pole dance. You know somewhere some lucky guy is setting the hook. But it's not you. Tip-ups, anyone?

Thus, there's a fine line between vicarious enjoyment and envy, a lesson I take with me as we embark on producing the *Buccaneers and Bones* TV series with the Bonefish and Tarpon Trust, celebrating bonefishing and the dreamy flats they inhabit. Our "set" is none other than Deep Water Cay, a destination created in 1958 by angling legend Gil Drake and *Field & Stream* fishing editor A.J. McLane. The duo embarked Ponce de Leon-like on a journey to uncover the greatest bonefishing in the Bahamas, which bears more than a small resemblance to finding the Fountain of Youth.

Legendary brothers of the flats—the late Lefty Kreh and the Bahamas' William Pinder—discussing the subtle tweaks to the perfect cast.

Their travels led to Deep Water Cay, a place with exactly the right mix of flats and nearby deep ocean shelves. They provide the optimal recipe to consistently support extraordinary numbers of bonefish on the flats, big bones at that. The constant circulation of water at the right temperature in these shallows allows them to fish longer than most places in the archipelago. That fact wasn't lost on the lodge's current owner either, Paul Vahldiek, a land and water conservationist and raconteur who is active from the Bahamas to the Rocky Mountains.

A generous supply of flats that haven't been over-fished and the sprawling compound of the lodge and its private cabins is an ideal venue to bring our celebrity cast of Hollywood and musical luminaries as well as fly-fishing sensei Lefty Kreh and veteran NBC News anchor Tom Brokaw. Kreh and Brokaw had never met until the series brought them together. Since the introduction, however, they became annual fishing pals, a friendship that became evident on camera through the years of filming the series.

If you doubt what vitality bonefish can bring to a soul, you should have spent a few minutes with Kreh who, in his late 80s at the time, greeted each morning on the flats like a child would a new playground. He brought hope to youngsters in their 60s and 70s who wanted to be doing what Kreh was at his age. *Perhaps he's the Fountain of Youth?* I pondered, watching him work a room of fly fishers like a politician in need of money.

Our production crew readies a literal boat load of equipment to film the exploits of the team's flats adventures. Meanwhile, I plan to sneak in a filming session of my own, sampling some of Deep Water's innumerable flats while the rest of the cast is still in makeup and ward-

It took three trips into the backing before this hefty bone finally surrendered.

Pound for pound there's no fish on our planet that delivers more fight than a bonefish.

robe. Taking me on the early morning tour is Meko, who in this community and among anglers who make the Bahamas a regular flats fishing stop, has reached celebrity status in his own right. In fact, like Cher or Prince, he goes by only one name anymore. When you see him stand atop a poling platform, scanning the flats for signs of life, it's clear that he was an osprey in an earlier life, hatched at one point before leaving the nest to spend the rest of his existence as a hunter of fish.

We slip off the dock quietly the first morning before the ensemble has left the confines of the lodge. Meko wants to hit the first flat just as the sun is high enough in the sky to pierce the surface glare and reveal the mirrored form of the bonefish, or at least their shadows cast on the sand beneath them. After a 30-minute run, we glide to a stop where Meko begins poling, scanning a baseball diamond-sized patch of water the way a submariner monitors sonar. It isn't long before he spies our first fish.

"Point your rod at 10 o'clock," he says. "Got 'em at 60 feet?"

I don't see the bones but give it a shot, feeling like Helen Keller fishing by Braille at the front of the skiff.

"They spooked—don't worry," he says.

"I'll take your word for it. I never saw them."

The bones are hungry and on the move, however, so it isn't long before we find a tailing school. He eases the boat about 50 feet from the pod, cocks the craft in perfect position for me to cast with the breeze quartering from behind. Three false casts and the Mantis Shrimp plunks like bonefish manna from heaven in front of the lead fish's nose. Apparently feeling blessed for the gift, the six-pound bone picks it up and heads to Bimini in a flash, doing to my reel what Hendrix did to a guitar. There are no sweeter notes to a flats angler.

Brokaw and McGuane don't let a slow day on the water bother them as much as does the guide.

"Way to go my man, you got 'em!"

A great flats guide is many things. Of course, he must possess raptor-like vision to see bones in all manner of light extremes. Then he has to have a nose to tell where the bonefish are going to be at any given weather and tidal condition. He must be able to size up his client and put him in position to reach a fish, no matter his casting skill. If he wants a decent tip, he needs to realize that while he lives on the flats and has honed his vision to pick up the subtle shape of a bonefish at great distance, his clients seldom possess the same ability.

Most of all, however, the great ones know they're blessed to be earning a living doing what others spend a lifetime making money to afford to do. Every time I've fished with Meko, it is as if he feels lucky for the opportunity and brings an enthusiasm to want to share his fishing prowess and good company. He lives by the mantra, "If you love what you do, you'll never work a day in your life." Then, suddenly, Meko snaps me out of my *musings on guiding* as we pole through the flat in search of more fish.

"Give me a cast: 50 feet at 10 o'clock. Strip . . . strip . . . *stop* . . . strip."

Bingo! The fish can't resist chasing the final strip. The strip, strip, *stop* . . . strip-the-fly-in cadence, when properly timed with a fish's reactions, is poison for bones, often tweaking them out of an otherwise indifferent posture. The key is being able to see the fish well enough to understand its relationship to the fly in the water. Did I say having the vision of a bird of prey is important to a flats guide?

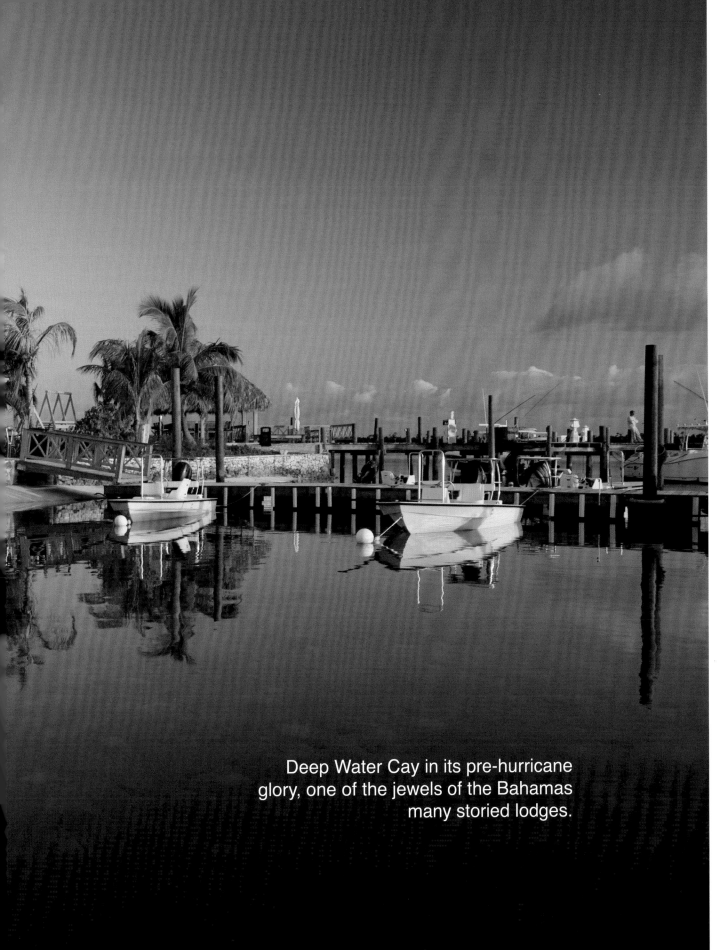

Deep Water Cay in its pre-hurricane
glory, one of the jewels of the Bahamas
many storied lodges.

The first time a trout fisherman hooks a bonefish an entire recalibration of fly fishing occurs. It did for me, anyway. Up until that moment, there is no way to know that a five-pound fish could possess such wicked strength and speed. I don't know who put them on the clock, but I've read that bonefish can swim upwards of 40 miles per hour, which seems a conservative estimate by my observations. Bonefish are piscatorial spark plugs that react to a hook the way a horse does a whip. If bonefish could jump they would never be landed. If they grew to 50 pounds they would rule the oceans.

"Point your rod straight off the bow," says Meko, once again interrupting my *flatsendental* meditation. "Little more left—shoot it 30 feet."

The bonefish picks up the fly on the move and makes three long runs, the third one interrupted by a nurse shark attracted by the commotion and looking for a snack. I put the wood to the fish to get it to the boat quickly in the hopes of saving it from the shark that wants to play surgeon. Meanwhile, Meko slaps his pole at the predator in an effort to spook it away.

A distressed bonefish leaves a scent trail that sharks follow like a bird dog might a pheasant. We take the four-pounder into the mangroves and release it there, a sanctuary too shallow for sharks. Once the fish regains its strength, it'll be ready to handle the usual predatory challenges found on these flats—perhaps the most savage ecosystem on our planet with scores of sharks, barracuda and needlefish lurking about.

Watching the friendship grow between the celebrity cast of our decade-long *Buccaneers & Bones* flats fishing series was one of the treasures of the experience. The series was produced in conjunction with the Bonefish & Tarpon Trust.

Bonefish and Tarpon Trust has done much research on bonefish survival rates after the catch and it's clear that the less you handle a bonefish and the quicker you release it—preferably never taking it out of the water—the greater its chance of survival. Even if you don't see sharks in the vicinity, rest assured that they are nearby and will detect the scent of a distressed fish quickly and come to investigate. In one study, upwards of 40 percent of permit tracked after being caught were subsequently eaten by sharks. I know what you're thinking: *That means maybe three or four permit a year are killed in this manner.*

The healthy waters around the Bahamas are resplendent with nurse, lemon and blacktip sharks among others. It's a testament to the conservation ethic embraced by the Bahamian government and its people as well as the efforts of BTT to help them realize the value of their fishery.

Like any morning on the water with Meko, it's one to remember—both for the fish and the company, for he's like sharing a boat with your own motivational life coach. As we pull up to the Deep Water dock for the afternoon shift change, I see that the vast flat past the dock is prime for bones owing to optimal incoming tides. There's still plenty of good light so I strike off to wade-fish the 300-acre flat, a gem of a fishery that we so often boat past en route to more distant waters. Not this time.

Liam Neeson getting ready for his close-up.

A quick release dramatically improves bonefish survival and experts now suggest keeping the fishing in the water during the entire process.

Tom Brokaw prepares to deliver
an invitation to a passing bone as
Lefty Kreh looks on.

I get about 150 yards from the dock, walking slowly and stopping periodically in one foot of water to scan, and I catch sight of a lone bone, its forked tail sticking out of the water maybe 80 feet ahead. It's a big fish, perhaps eight pounds, judging by the size of the tail. It's swimming toward me so I kneel on the flat and wait for it to hit my range. The line between fishing and hunting is suddenly blurred, for the sensation is no different than waiting for a bull elk to step out from behind a juniper and present a shot. As the bone hits 60 feet, I begin false casting some 15 feet to the side of it, simply trying to gauge the amount of line I'll need to put the Crazy Charlie ahead of the fish's nose.

With my crude measurement complete, I adjust the cast to drop the fly in front of the moving fish. My low angle makes it difficult to tell exactly how close the fish is to my fly, but I make two short strips hoping the movement will catch the attention of the bone. Nothing. I let it sit for a few seconds and strip once more . . . *wham!*

The fish rips 100 feet of line off the reel in the time that it takes me to stand from my kneeling position. It makes two extraordinarily long runs, well into the backing, before we finally meet. No matter the size (sure enough, about eight pounds), it is an epic encounter and an altogether intoxicating moment on the flats. A solo wade fish is worth five from a boat to me. There is an elemental satisfaction in having stalked a big bone and successfully brought it to hand.

Therein lies much of the magic of bonefishing, and it is just such encounters that transform anglers into conservation advocates, for once bitten we cannot imagine letting such an experience evaporate. Even if you're a Midwest walleye angler, you're still part of that enduring tribe called anglers, the people who speak for all fish and their waters.

Who knows, maybe you'll one day wade these same flats, and wouldn't it be nice if the fish were still here? 🌎

This is how Patagonia's Yvon Chouinard prefers to social distance.

What to Bring

Rods and reels: 6- to 8-weight

Lines: Weight-forward floating

Flies: Crabs, Charlies, Gotchas and the Meko Special

Other Essential Gear: Polarized lenses and brimmed hat

Don't Forget to Pack: Your passport—can clear customs at the private airstrip

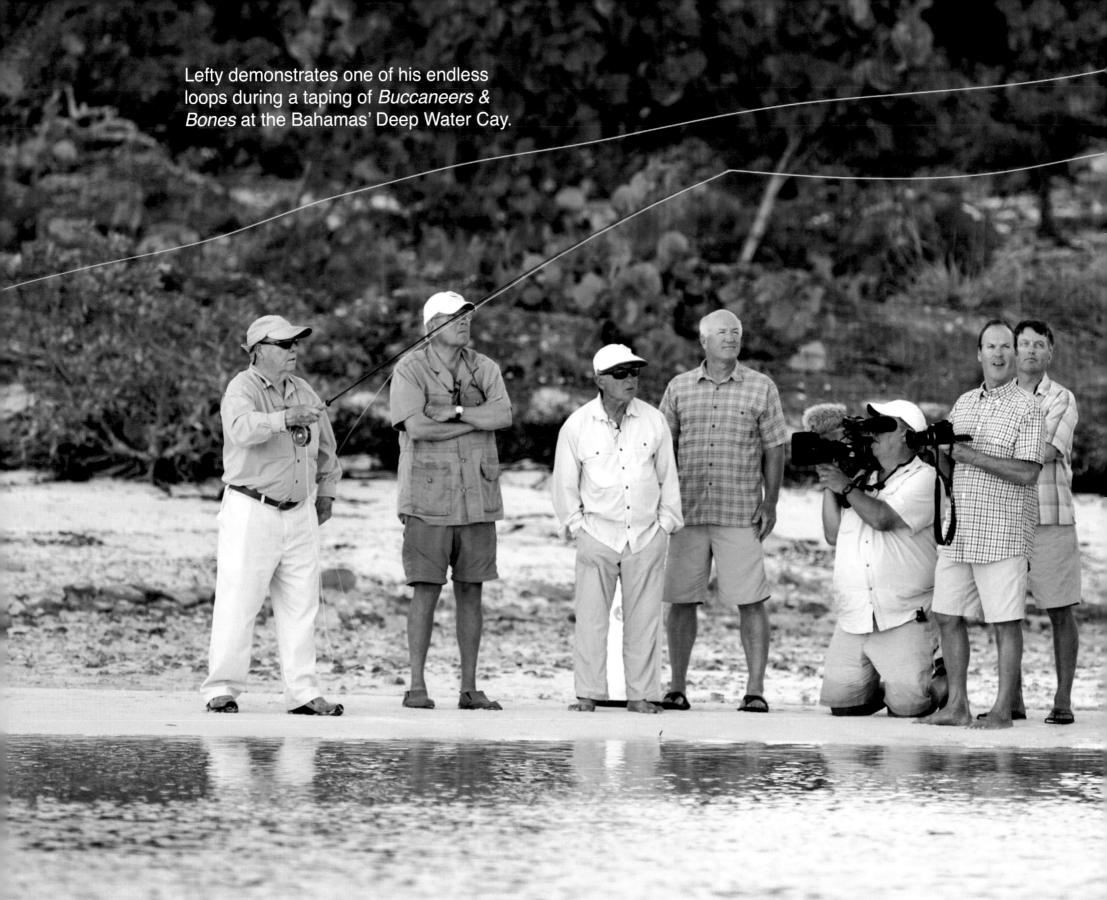

Lefty demonstrates one of his endless loops during a taping of *Buccaneers & Bones* at the Bahamas' Deep Water Cay.

There are a wealth of flats surrounding Deep Water, a destination the legendary Gil Drake discovered after spending many years in search of the best bonefish angling.

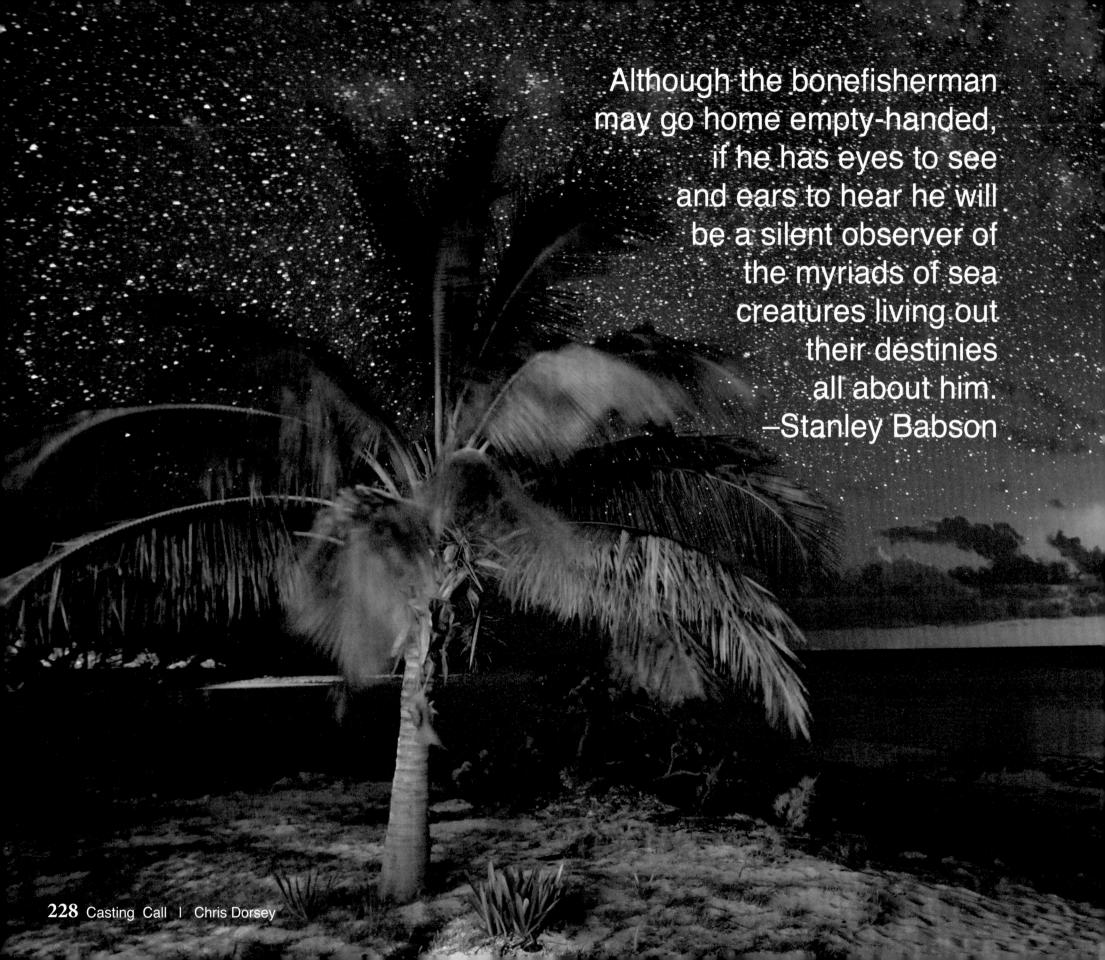

Although the bonefisherman
may go home empty-handed,
if he has eyes to see
and ears to hear he will
be a silent observer of
the myriads of sea
creatures living out
their destinies
all about him.
—Stanley Babson

A fish that gets away always carries
some insoluble secret with him.
– Roderick Haig-Brown

Michael Keaton holds a lighting rod as a tarpon mesmerizes our crew in an electric moment during the taping of *Buccaneers & Bones*.

Anchor Away

On Assignment With Tom Brokaw In Belize

Take the cause of saving the tropical saltwater flats ecosystem, add a worthwhile conservation organization in need of awareness and introduce a famous cast willing to help. Those were the ingredients that conspired to create a decade-long television series with the tongue-in-cheek title of *Buccaneers and Bones.*

The programs have been seen over most of the free world and even a few communist states—just to remind the poor bastards what they're missing. The business approach was part of a winning formula developed over years of avoiding honest work: support our planet, help give a worthy cause identity, have some fun along the way and get someone else to pay for it. The last part being the most important. Check, check, check . . . and check's in the mail.

The concept of the series was simple: celebrate memorable flats fishing throughout the Caribbean and beyond, the focus area of the south Florida-based non-profit called Bonefish and Tarpon Trust. So little is known about the importance and fragility of these ocean nurseries that BTT was formed by some friends at Ocean Reef, a community that sits between Key Largo and heaven (closer to heaven) to raise money to study these fish and the ecological ribbon where salt and turf meet. It's amazing what can be accomplished over cocktails and dinner when people such as Tom Davidson, Russ Fisher, Adelaide Skoglund and Bill Legg—some of the founders of the organization—get together to figure out how to save the Earth . . . or at least their little piece of it.

Each season, we identified a new region to showcase, selecting a lodge to house our cast of angling A-listers that included Tom Brokaw, Michael Keaton, Huey Lewis, Liam Neeson, Jimmy Kimmel, Patagonia founder Yvon Chouinard, novelist Tom McGuane, Jim Belushi, Lefty Kreh and many others.

Keys permit guide Will Benson does a mind-meld with one of the few permit ever caught during the filming of *Buccaneers & Bones*.

It's 5 o'clock here as I catch up with Brokaw over a beer and listen to one of his countless stories having worked the front-lines of history as NBC News anchor for more than 20 years.

Seeing well-known individuals sharing a passion for fishing became a lure to attract angling audiences and, by extension, supporters of BTT's work.

One thing you learn when producing such a series is that celebrity is a funny and oftentimes fickle thing. People tend to live in worlds of their making, constructs they create built around passions, their pool of friends, the entertainment they seek, the sports they love and the like. I recall shooting one season for the series at Bair's Lodge, one of the Nervous Waters properties on South Andros. I was waiting at a nearby dock for my flats boat to arrive for a day of fishing and filming when a couple of local guides not affiliated with our shoot approached me.

"Are you part of the group filming the TV show?"

"I am."

"Love that show, man—who's fishing this season?"

"We've got Huey Lewis . . . Jim Belushi . . . Jimmy Kimmel . . . Yvon Chouinard. . . Tom McGuane . . . Lefty Kreh . . . ." He cuts me off.

"Lefty f---ing Kreh is on the island?"

I'm certain the man would have traded a week of guiding for the chance to meet Lefty. In his mind, there are two folks who can walk on water: Lefty—and some guy named Jesus.

This season we are headed to Belize and Turneffe Flats, a sprawling lodge compound on Belize's Turneffe Atoll, the country's largest marine reserve. It's a Caribbean getaway famous for its ready access to productive flats fishing as well as diving and snorkeling. We are here to see about the bonefish and permit and judge for ourselves in the fishing is as good as the rumors of it.

Patagonia's Bill Klyn demonstrates the perfect bonefish release.

I join Brokaw as we strike off with guide Dion Young to explore one of countless flats a short boat ride from the lodge. Brokaw's been a fly fisherman much of his life and his ranch on Montana's West Boulder River gives him as much practice as his challenging schedule will allow. Still, pitching to trout in a small mountain stream is the minor leagues of casting; the flats demand more. Whenever I head to bonefish waters, I tend to spend the first day of the trip working the rust off my cast, trying to get my double-haul timing down to deliver a fly to a bonefish's nose at 60 feet, instead of the back of my head.

I've known Brokaw for several years, mostly owing to the TV biz and a shared passion for chasing fish and fowl. I always wonder what occupies the mind of a man who has been on the front lines of history for much of his adult life, more than 20 years at the anchor's desk of NBC News. How does the stimulation of covering wars, meetings between Gorbachev and Reagan and standing on the rubble of what was formerly the Berlin Wall compare to finding a fish the size of a calf muscle?

There's always one guy in the room that has an "I-didn't-see-that-one-coming" story. Brokaw is always that guy. There was a shoot, early in the production of the series, when we parked our fishing notables in a semi-circle of chairs. We just wanted to get them talking and see if there were any gems to be mined later in post. I simply asked them to share their favorite fishing story. Keaton went first, followed by McGuane, Chouinard pleaded the fifth, then Brokaw said something that tied geopolitics into catching a permit in Belize and we were all slightly bedazzled by the story. Then it was Lefty's turn.

"I remember fishing with Castro and Hemingway in Cuba," he starts, as matter of fact as a peanut butter sandwich. "I probably should have paid more attention to what Castro and Hemingway were talking about but I was too busy trying to figure out how the hell our guide was tying the mackerel on the hook so that we could catch marlin."

A night stroll through the Belizean forest uncovered this beauty.

As we ease along a bank of mangroves, Brokaw is up first and is doing some dry casts to straighten out his line and smooth his cadence before there's a bonefish in sight. It isn't long, however, and he's getting instructions from Young who is perched like a pelican on the edge of his poling platform.

"There he is . . . 10 o'clock . . . 50 feet . . . big bonefish . . . look at the size of that one!"

What looks like the dorsal fin of a small shark knifes out of the surface. Then its tail forks out of the water as it feeds in case we aren't already aware that this is a brute. Nothing like starting with a nine-pounder out of the gate—no pressure, Brokaw, I think to myself.

The South Dakota kid delivers a strike and the fish takes it. *I'll be damned.* It changes zip codes in an instant, the reel searing as if it's going to spin off the rod. While much of the work of the encounter has been done to this point, third base isn't the same as home plate. There's still time for rejection. What could possibly go wrong, you ask? How 'bout stepping on the line? Wrapping the line around the reel? A wind knot snagging a rod guide? Loose line hooking a cooler snap? Need I go on?

Lefty couldn't make one of our shoots in Belize but there were signs of him every-where...literally.

Note that Keaton and the tarpon
are sporting similar looks...
it's hard telling which one was
more surprised by the meeting.

Brokaw focuses on the task at hand. There's no premature celebration because he knows the possible sources of error are endless and, in any instant, his line could dangle like a participle. When the fish reaches the boat, the beast of a bone brings a memory and conversation starter that will play out in all its glory later at the lodge. If not for the evidence of film, this would surely be a 12-pounder. Indeed, when I was just a magazine writer—not a TV host—I used to catch much bigger fish.

"When you make a great cast and hook up, it is rewarding beyond my ability to describe it," says Brokaw. "Because when they grab it . . . BANG! they're gone." That answers the question, I guess, about how meeting a bonefish compares to greeting Gorbachev.

Therein lies the magic of bonefish, for if the fish could look in a mirror they would undoubtedly see a barracuda. They swim the way a peregrine dives, traveling so quickly through water that they can move faster than the human eye's ability to track them—shadow or no shadow. All that's left is the rumor of a fish and a sand contrail in the water. If your fly is in a fish's mouth as it streaks off, you'll be witness to what amounts to the angling world's hit and run.

"If you tied the tail of a 10-pound bass to the tail of a 10-pound bonefish," Lefty once told me, "the bonefish would strip the scales off the bass pulling it backward." His teachings are often illustrative.

As Lefty Kreh once said, "If you can't have fun with Huey Lewis, you belong in a cemetery."

One of the most rewarding parts of producing Bucs and Bones for so many years was seeing the friendship—kinship, really—develop between Brokaw and Lefty. The duo became fast friends and found plenty of reasons to get together apart from the series taping. I once had the two of them to my place on Montana's Big Hole River. Lefty was non-denominational when it came to fishing pursuits—though nothing surpassed his fascination with bonefishing, for it gave him an excuse to hang with the people he most enjoyed.

With Brokaw basking in the glow of his recent bonefish performance, it is my turn to step up and see what the fish gods might deliver my way. It is mere minutes before a single bone, a hefty one at that, begins nosing its way out of the mangroves toward us. When it hits 60 feet, I give it a shrimp fly and the fish accepts the invitation, shooting parallel along the mangroves until it decides to use my fly line to tie a bow around some stems sticking out of the water. That's when a really good guide will think quickly, hop out of the boat and untangle the line, which is exactly what our captain does. The strong fish makes it to the leader--a handsome seven-pounder that fights like he could have been closer to 10. Video again ruins what could have been yet another Moby-Dick moment.

Brokaw picks up a few more fish and I do the same before we return to the lodge and reconnect with the rest of the traveling troupe of castaways. As we enter the lodge, Huey Lewis is holding court, obsessing over his new quest to land a permit. Clearly, it is his new drug and he's in need of a fix. As luck would have it, there are few places better than Belize to find the species.

Keaton has supported many conservation causes throughout his illustrious acting career. He's both a good fisherman and a fun addition to any troupe.

An arrival briefing for our crew…
it was as exhilarating as it looks,
but necessary nonetheless.

The next day, I join Lewis for a permit hunt. The morning breaks partly cloudy and mostly gray, with a good bit of wind…maybe 15- to 20- mile-per-hour gusts. We're going to have to see the fish's sword like tail sticking out of the water if we hope to find one, for the deeper water is margarita murky in the muted light. If there's one thing that's never in short supply with Lewis, however, it's enthusiasm—no matter the weather.

An hour into our three-hour tour we spot a pair of fins 60 yards to our left, moving parallel with our boat. The fish look like they're cruising to a new location but they are the only permit we've seen all morning so we ease that way—about 70 feet distant—when Lewis gives them, what else, the news, making a solid cast about 10 feet ahead of them.

"That's perfect . . . wait . . . strip now," says our guide.

Nothing.

"Damn, what did I do wrong?" asks Lewis.

"Nothing, man . . . that's permit fishing."

In 10 years of fishing for this series, only a handful of permit were ever caught on camera. In one case—season eight or nine—we had to bring in a ringer, famous south Florida permit guide Will Benson, so we could prove to viewers that the species would actually take a fly. Up until then, the notion seemed purely theoretical.

ewis never did connect with a permit on that trip, but the permit hooked him. He's since gone on to land his hard-won permit. Lefty Kreh went to fish the flats on the other side, undoubtedly improving St. Peter's back cast. Brokaw continues to fail retirement, writing another book and training a new Lab. Keaton is winning every acting award but wishing he could spend more time on the water. Chouinard continues to practice social distancing, usually with a fly rod. And Montana trout and Florida tarpon have joint custody of McGuane.

It's a wrap.

What to Bring

For Bonefish

Rods: Nine-foot four-piece for 8-weight

Reels: Saltwater reel holding at least 150 yards of 20-pound backing

Lines: Weight-forward floating

Flies: Pop's Bonefish Bitters, Crazy Charlies, EP Micro Crab

For Permit

Rod: 9-weight or 10=weight

Reel: Saltwater reel holding at least 200 yards of 20-pound backing

Line: Weight-floating, 10 feet of leader, 1X to 0X tippet

Flies: Del Brown's Permit Crab, Raghead Crab, EP Permit Crab

For Tarpon

Rods: 11- or 12-weight

Reels: Saltwater reel holding at least 150 yards of 30-pound backing

Lines: Full-sinking clear Type I Intermediate

Flies: Every fly is good as long as it is black and purple

Other Essential Gear: Thick-soled wading boots

Don't Forget to Pack: Reef-safe sunscreen SPF 50 or stronger

Klyn (orange) and Matt Connolly in the never ending search for tailing bones.

The first decent fish of any species a kid catches is the Big One and you don't forget it any more than you forget the first girl in your life.
—Robert F. Jones

Yvon Chouinard living
the Patagonia brand
in Belize.

Chouinard would rather be wading a flat than casting from a boat...and he'd just as soon be alone as be listening to a guide.

Tarpon are an ancient species and their kind swimming today are the genetic survivors honed through millions of years of trial.

It pays to get out early before the wind kicks up as the bones ride a rising tide in search of breakfast.

Taking A Bight Out Of Andros

Welcoming The Bain Of Your Existence At Mangrove Cay

We're floating in a watercolor world of pastels: Liquid turquoise that give way to skies as blue as Marilyn Monroe's eyes and just as seductive. A slight breeze keeps us cool but doesn't impede our casts. It's a vision of bonefishing perfection in the Bahamas. To be more specific, we're casting about the famed Middle Bight of Andros Island, a destination that tweaks bonefishing fanatics the way mentioning Montana's Bighorn or Chile's Futaleufu to a trout angler invariably stirs their hackles.

It's early the first morning of the trip and I'm standing at the bow with rod in one hand and Gotcha in the other . . . and a pocketful of enthusiasm. All around us, the flats are waking up as the tide is sneaking into the mangroves the way a fog rolls in—*on cat feet*, as Sandburg wrote—signaling the bones to follow into the cover where breakfast is being served.

"Give me a cast—9 o'clock. Fifty feet. Strip . . . *stop* . . . strip . . . strip . . . *stop*," murmurs Marvin Miller, a 20-something Bahamian guide whom I didn't take for a minimalist when I boarded his craft. I cannot see the fish but cast as instructed. He's perched six feet above me, peering ahead like a fish eagle able to see the stage before us clearly while it remains mostly cloaked for me. He has a front-row seat to every missed opportunity and blown cast I make. I begin to subconsciously calculate how much tip will be needed at the end of the day for hush money.

At first, the fishing feels like casting by sonar, for no manner of polarized lenses can help you see what the best Bahamian guides seem to sense through intuition. I'm casting on faith, trusting Miller at his word that there are indeed bones approaching. In a few seconds, with my fly waiting at the bottom of the flat somewhere in the vicinity of approaching fish, I finally spy the shadows of the fish torpedoing toward us. I see them just in time to watch a plump Andros bone suck the fly and turn and run to deeper water as if late for an appointment somewhere in Cuba.

Codd is about to strip-set yet another bone.

Much has been written and said about the reel-hissing initial run of a bonefish. From my experience, most of those descriptions have been a bit trite. The phenomenon simply stretches the English language's ability to communicate it's awesomeness, for the fish—pound for pound—has no rival. I'm left with maybe five or six rotations on my backing before the bone gives me a chance to recover—all the line disappearing in a matter of mere seconds. When hooked, the fish swim faster than you can track; all that's left as evidence of the hookup is a cloud of sand lingering in the water. Three times I reel the fish within sight of the boat and in each instance the bone strips my reel clean as I begin to feel like Charlie Brown about to kick a football. At the jolt of each run, my line rips out of the water as if the fish is going to tow us to sea.

At last, I wrestle the eight-pound fish to the boat and look at it in sheer wonder given what it was just able to do to my rod and reel, as if it must have had an accomplice for its dine-and-dash routine. For the first-time visitor to the flats, what becomes readily apparent during a bonefish baptism is that this isn't going to be like another trip to catch a freshwater species. Forget the trout guide's mantra that it isn't the distance of your cast that counts, just accuracy and how you work the fly. On the flats, distance *and* accuracy both matter, as does the ability to deliver a fly in a hurry. Bonefishing is hunting with a fly rod and the roaming fish won't wait for you to make a half-dozen false casts in order to place the fly. No two words better epitomize bone-fishing than *double haul*.

The crew at Mangrove Cay are all smiles (mostly). The pleasant nature of the Bahamian people is one of the great draws of this island nation.

Mangrove Cay is a beautiful, well-appointed destination that sits within easy boat rides of excellent bonefishing.

The next morning, Sharad Williams, a 22-year old Bahamian, pilots my boat to the west side of Andros, famous for hosting the largest fish in the archipelago. It's another blessedly calm day in which the water becomes a mirror of the sky, one quicksilver abyss with no defining line between water and heaven. The bight is rimmed by mangroves, their spider leg roots webbing into the limestone island. They give Bob Ross texture to a world otherwise dominated by shades of surreal blue and aquamarine.

Williams steers the boat to a favorite flat bisected by a tidal stream that looks like an artery running through a football field-sized sandbox covered in calf-deep water. It is something of a dance hall for bonefish, and I am ready for the party to commence. As soon as Williams climbs aboard the poling platform, he spies a pair of bones nosing the bottom for crabs 50 feet ahead of us in the manner of a Lab trolling a dinner table. I drop the fly two feet ahead of one of the fish and the other one pounces on it before turning to run out of sight in an instant. Three runs into my backing later and I release the four-pounder, wondering if I came equipped to handle one of the 10-pound fish for which this side of the island is so famous.

"Two o'clock . . . moving right to left . . . give me all ya got, mon," says Williams as a trio of bones cross some 50 feet out. I pitch the fly slightly behind and short of the fish but don't spook them, so I pick the line back up as gently as possible and lay the fly on their noses with my second attempt. The three fish dart toward the fly. The first to

Liz Bain sets the bar high when it comes to running a bonefishing lodge—attention to detail is a mantra here.

arrive picks it up and runs 200 feet before spitting the hook scarcely in the time it takes to utter, "Fish on!" I stand jaw agape with one fly in the sand and one apparently zipped open.

This flat is alive with bones. I reload and begin scanning once again as Williams propels us through the shallows. Maybe five minutes later, we cruise up to a bone holding steady at 30 feet as though it's plugged into some cosmic electrical socket, undoubtedly recharging for upcoming sprints. When my fly plops next to him, he spins around and devours it as if pleased that such an appetizing morsel would suddenly appear from the heavens. Once again my 8-weight arcs to the water, bending steadily under the strain of the bolting bonefish. The fish is a mere three pounds but he doesn't know he's small. It's almost as if there's an inverse correlation: the smaller the bone the harder they fight. Apparently even fish can have Napoleon complexes.

Before leaving Williams's favorite haunt, he spies another group of bones at 80 feet and crossing: "Twelve o'clock . . . moving left to right . . . deeze are double-digit bones, mon . . . give it to 'em!"

Dinner anyone? We have shrimp and crab on the menu...and plenty of them.

Ready...set...go!
If any species of fish
were built for speed
it is the bonefish.

Codd versus bonefish on one of the many wade flats found near Mangrove Cay.

Signs of life are everywhere on the flats.

We averaged a dozen bones per day during our stay with a good mix of hard-fighting four to six pounders.

While I can see the fish, I can't quite reach them with the cast. It's like a nightmare where you can't ever quite reach an object of obsession, stuck at third base, as it were. The fish cruise out of sight and into my dreams where I'll remember them the next time I look at my fly box half-full of tattered Gotchas. I hook nine bones in all, a passable day on Andros, and we return to Mangrove Cay, a delightful lodge run impeccably by Liz Bain, an enterprising and resourceful woman whose vision and sweat equity has helped create a bucket-list destination.

There's time for a couple of sundowners and a small mountain of stone crab before easing off to a dinner of lobster Thermidor, perhaps the club's most popular attraction outside of 10-pound bonefish. Tomorrow we will head offshore for dorado, then maybe to the South Bight for tarpon . . . or perhaps we'll go back to the west for more bones. Such are the dilemmas of a place most anglers have come to know simply as Fantasy Island. 🌐

What to Bring

Rods: 8-weight for bonefish, 10-weight for tarpon

Reels: Reels with good drag and a large arbor

Lines: Bonefish lines with a neutral fly line color

Flies: Variety of traditional bonefish flies—there is no turtle grass so you don't need weedless flies

Other Essential Gear: Neoprene flats boots

Don't Forget to Pack: Polarized lenses

There are plenty of double digit bones swimming the flats around Andros.

No one is ever late for dinner at Mangrove Cay.

This bone looks as if it could swim over a caesar salad.

As a seller of fishing dreams, Codd gets plenty of time on the water and knows of what he speaks.

Ascension Bay is one of the world's richest bonefish waters.

Bay Watch

Forecasting The Yucatan: Mostly Bonefish With A Slight Chance Of Permit

Audomaro Chuc poles our skiff through a narrow channel lined by impenetrable mangrove hedges that create a water-bound maze. Solve the riddle of the labyrinth and your reward will be a plethora of hungry bonefish. About the time we seem hopelessly lost, we round a final turn and emerge in an open pool some 50 yards wide and 200 yards long. The water is crystalline but is tinted emerald by the turtle grass waving dreamingly in the current below.

Everywhere we scan, schools of bonefish glide gently as though we've discovered El Dorado. I instinctively begin to false cast as my eyes dart around looking for the perfect landing spot for my mantis shrimp imitation. A school of 40 fish is but 50 feet away, so I cast to the near edge of the aggregate. The instant the fly breaks the surface tension of the water, the fish scatter in all directions like shards from a crystal glass hitting a tile floor.

The reaction serves as a quick reminder that even isolated bonefish have little tolerance for ham-handed fly deliveries. I pitch three more times to now more distant bones only to watch the fish continue their departure. Sufficiently humbled, I surrender the bow to my wife Amy as she unleashes her double-haul. Her cast is more delicate than mine, but still the fish show no interest in either of our offerings. Eventually, we manage to rid the entire pool of every fish save for a handful of bluegill-sized mangrove snapper that appear to relish their newfound solitude.

"We go to new spot," says Chuc, having seen enough rejection for one location.

We wind our way through another serpentine trail to a new flat: a vast expanse of turquoise-colored water that seems especially spacious given the tight quarters we just abandoned. The flat is part of a sweeping lagoon created by a three-mile-long isthmus of land that juts down the Caribbean coast of Mexico's Yucatan Peninsula like some long-forgotten Mayan breakwater.

We are fishing the waters near Boca Paila Lodge, a decades-old fishing monastery of sorts, home to an ancient order of anglers. The lagoon is resplendent with a diverse cast of game fish, including bones, tarpon, permit, snook, barracuda and myriad other species with lesser credits. There are numerous other fishermen in the area: osprey, herons, egrets, crocodiles and local lobstermen to name but a few. Our flats boat provides a window into a natural amphitheater where the links of the food chain are visible in all their splendor. The lodge's fishing waters lie within the Sian Ka'an Biosphere Reserve, a place that halted all commercial netting in 1986, preserving a snapshot of what was once common throughout the Yucatan.

Chuc poles us onto a baseball diamond-sized flat that is especially shallow, perhaps no more than 10 or 12 inches deep. I scan back and forth for the subtle forms of bones whose shadows are often more visible than the fish themselves—here one instant and gone the next depending on available light. I slip into a flats hypnosis of sorts, the combination of waves and 95-degree heat sending me into a momentary transcendental state. I turn to stare at the nearby mangroves to recalibrate my eyes before returning back to my bay watch.

"Bonefeesh . . . 2 o'clock . . . 60 feet," says Chuc as he punches his push pole into the mud to turn the boat as a defensive measure against my back cast. I uncoil 50 feet in four false casts and let the loaded rod shoot the remaining line three feet in front of the cruising bone. It darts toward the fly. I twitch the fly slightly. The fish hovers over the offering for an instant and then streaks off with the hook imbedded in the top of its lip and its engine revved in top gear. If these fish were the size of pike, they'd never be landed with anything less than a harpoon.

Amy returns to the bow, determined to catch her first-ever bonefish. She's a veteran of countless trout streams, but despite my counsel that casting to bones bears as much resemblance to trout fishing as it does panning for gold, she shoots me a look of, "If you can do it. . . ."

I've met few people in my life who enjoy fishing as much as Amy.

First morning on the dock brings a delicious mix of anticipation and euphoria with the looming prospect of flats full of bones.

She has spent several weeks casting in a park near our home, working the Bermuda as if it were a flat at low tide. Despite such practice, the combination of a moving boat, cruising bonefish and over eagerness to want to connect serves to undermine her casting stroke.

"Don't rush," I suggest, "take your time."

She ignores me, choosing instead to concentrate on the water ahead as if my words were lost in the breeze. Soon another bone emerges, this time only 30 feet away. She flips the rod back and forth like the tail of a jubilant pup. The line never has a chance to catch up and she creates the mother of all knots. Fish and opportunity slip away.

"You must slow down," says Chuc, "feel the line go back before you throw ahead."

Amy immediately does as Chuc instructs. The results are astonishing, an effortless cast that zips 60 feet as though it could have gone 100.

"He's a good instructor," she proclaims with the same tone she uses to compliment other women's husbands who do things that I don't: fix cars, build additions, fly airplanes, etc.

As Lefty Kreh once said to me many years later, "Chris, I can teach any person on Earth to fly fish—except my wife."

I ignore the bait as I can hear Amy snicker under her breath. Instead, I step up to the bow and help her scan the flat because, of course, a woman needs all the help she can get when fishing for bones.

"Ten o'clock!" says Chuc as though we were stalking unicorns and this was the first he'd ever seen. Amy pitches the fly 30 feet, just four feet in front of a pair of approaching bones. The two fish race to the mini Gotcha that sits on the bottom, the winner tearing off with the fly to the far end of the cove in mere seconds. There's nothing so unforgettable in an angler's life as the feel of a bonefish run for the first time. The fish takes the line to the backing three times before rolling to its side as Chuc plucks the fly from its mouth, releasing it to fight another day.

We escape the mid-afternoon heat by returning to our private cottage for a shower and margarita on Boca Paila's palm-lined beach. Other anglers return about the same time, including two visiting from Maine, Jim Kaiser and Laurie Carle. Both have just caught permit, the Holy Grail of fly-fishing. It was an especially impressive feat for Carle who had never before been to the flats and had yet to even catch a bonefish. Up until that moment, I quite liked them.

Codd casts to a pair of permit working the edge of the mangroves.

There's one seat left...for you.

Amy and I opt to try for permit the last day of our stay, hoping, of course, that lightning would strike twice. Our guide is Audomaro's brother, Victor.

"Permit today," I say as we board his flats boat. Victor just smiles, lights a smoke and pulls the cord to rev his Yamaha outboard before I can utter any more ridiculousness. It was as if I'd asked to see a dodo. He pilots the skiff to the Boca, or opening of the lagoon that spills into the Caribbean.

"We see many permit here," he says before punctuating the remark by shrugging his shoulders and lifting his hands in the air as if to say *seeing them doesn't mean you'll catch 'em*. About the time I finish stripping 70 feet of line onto the deck, I spot a pair of permit working the bottom like swine rooting for truffles. The fish are moving along the edge of the mangroves from left to right. We're still 70 feet away, but I drop the crab fly 20 feet ahead of them. I'm hoping the fish continue their course and I'll simply twitch the crab ever so slightly as they get near it. The conclusion of the fantasy, of course, is that the permit will suck the fly in its mouth and take me into the backing 10 times before coming to net.

Instead, they ignore the fly as though it is little more than a pimple on a mullet's tail. The scenario continues most of the day, with us recording two follows as if we're muskie fishermen figure-eighting our jerk baits back to the boat.

As impossible as it seems, we return to the lodge and listen to more reports of permit being caught—a total of five among the six anglers in camp. My excuse for not catching a permit? The bones got in the way, of course.

Next time. . . . 🌀

What to Bring

Rods and Reels: 9-weight works for bonefish, permit, and tarpon

Lines: Floating line with tapered leaders

Flies: No. 6 and 8 bonefish flies, crabs for permit, toads and streamers for tarpon

Other Essential Gear: flats shoes with wading socks

Don't Forget to Pack: Lightweight, long sleeve, sunproof clothing

This is why you should always apply sunscreen.

The ruins of the bio-reserve are home to stunning Mayan structures. Few people know that the Mayan civilization ended because no one could catch a permit.

Codd with one of his
umpteen bonefish.

The last cast before returning to the lodge and dinner.

THE FUTURE

Nate Dorsey, Brays Island, South Carolina 2020

Parents don't frame photos of their kids playing video games. —Author Unknown

Luke Dorsey, Zambezi River 2016